MY
FOUR SEASONS
in FRANCE

Also by Janine Marsh

My Good Life in France

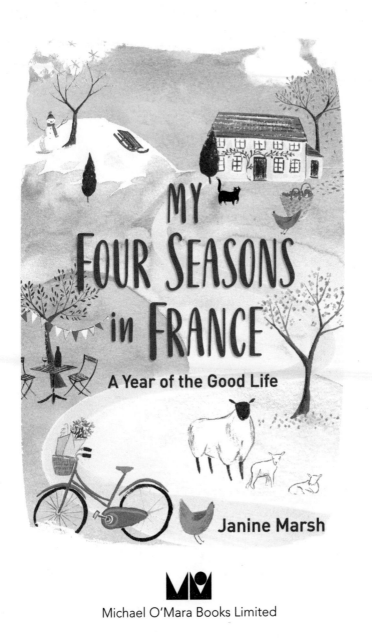

MY FOUR SEASONS in FRANCE

A Year of the Good Life

Janine Marsh

Michael O'Mara Books Limited

To Mark, who made me take a leap of faith.

'We travel not to escape life, but for life not to escape us.'

First published in Great Britain in 2020
by Michael O'Mara Books Limited
9 Lion Yard
Tremadoc Road
London SW4 7NQ

A CIP catalogue record for this book is available from the British Library.

Papers used by Michael O'Mara Books Limited are natural, recyclable products made from wood grown in sustainable forests. The manufacturing processes conform to the environmental regulations of the country of origin.

ISBN: 978-1-78929-047-9 in paperback print format
ISBN: 978-1-78929-048-6 in ebook format

1 2 3 4 5 6 7 8 9 10

www.mombooks.com

Cover illustration by Emma Block

Designed and typeset by K. DESIGN, Winscombe, Somerset

Printed and bound by CPI Group (UK) Ltd, Croydon, CR0 4YY

Contents

Prologue

IT ALL BEGAN on a freezing February day in 2004. My husband Mark and I had embarked on a day trip to Calais to buy wine with my dad, Frank, who had taken to drinking way too much whisky in order to drown his sorrows after my mum died a couple of years earlier. He was utterly lost without the love of his life and had taken to counting every day he had been without her. Whenever we spoke, he would say, 'You know, it's been four hundred days since your mother died,' and so on. It was so clear to me how much he thought of her and missed her every day, and I worried about him constantly. I thought that wine would be an improvement for him over the hard stuff, and that a trip with us might cheer him up a bit. And where better to pick up some wine than in France?

That morning, we picked up Dad from his home, not too far from ours in south-east London, and drove down to Dover, where we boarded a ferry to France under a wretched, ominously grey sky. The miserable weather certainly didn't improve when we reached Calais, with a gale coming in from the English Channel and buffeting the coast. After we had bought our wine, we decided to head inland from the coast to find somewhere cosy for lunch. We stopped off in the little town of Hesdin in the Seven Valleys, which, judging by the map, looked like it would be big enough to offer a grand choice of restaurants. Cobbled streets glistened under a steady stream of sleet as, wrapped up against the chilly wind, we searched for a place to eat. Alas we were too late. We didn't know it then, but restaurants in France are generally not an all-day affair and arriving at 1.30 p.m. will likely result in a '*non*' when you want a table.

'Blimey,' said Dad, 'you wouldn't want to live here, would you?'

En route back to the car, soggy and fed up, we passed many cafés and bistros that looked teasingly tempting, with their warm glowing lights and oh-so-French menus. As we stopped to look at houses for sale in an estate agent's window, the agent inside must have spotted our miserable, frozen faces and so he invited us in for coffee. It was too much of an enticement for my coffee-loving dad, and we trotted in behind him.

We were warmed by his generosity and the cosy interior of the shop, so the agent seized his chance: 'Ow much moanee are you looking to spend?' he asked.

I choked on the strong French coffee and assured him we had no money and we weren't looking for a house in France. Refusing to accept that we weren't interested in buying, the agent used every ounce of charm he could muster, and after realizing we were too poor to buy a house that didn't need completely doing up, he pulled out his three cheapest properties. He worked so hard to persuade us that I gave in and, thanking him for the coffee, took the details and bade him *au revoir*, certain we would never see him again.

Back in the car, we considered going straight home. 'Or … we could just take a look at these houses. They're all under a hundred thousand euros,' I said. Buying a house in France wasn't something I'd considered. But, a whole house for less than £60,000 – you couldn't get a garage in London for that. I was intrigued. And the agent was a good salesman, piquing my interest with his descriptions of vaulted cellars, wood-panelled lounges and 'bedrooms suitable for a queen'.

My suggestion was met with silence in the car. I wasn't sensing a great deal of enthusiasm from either of them. 'They're all in towns close to Hesdin. There might be a café open in one of them, and it's on the way back to Calais anyway, via the scenic route,' I continued.

Tempted by the prospect of a local café that might serve hot food, the unhappy men caved in to my suggestion. We drove for thirty minutes and arrived in a town that had a single road and a town hall, but no café. The house for sale was in a semi-derelict state.

In the next town, there were just a few houses on a single road. On peering through the windows of the apparently 'fit for royalty' house we could see that the walls, ceilings and even the doors were covered in hideous 1970s linoleum. It looked like a serial killer's den.

The last house was in a tiny village with no shops, no bars and no sign of life. I was starting to think that driving here to view a house we didn't want and couldn't afford, even though it cost less than a Hermès handbag, was probably a bit mad. By now, both Dad and Mark were seriously fed up.

I got out of the car to peer through a broken gate set into an unattractive concrete wall. Behind the wall was a very long and low detached farmhouse-style building with drab grey walls and a concrete-block extension. Paint was peeling from the windows and door, and the rain, pelting down on the moss-covered roof, spilled over gutters and gushed from a broken drainpipe. The rain-sodden front garden was filled with piles of broken bricks and rubble. The house looked abandoned.

'Let's just go,' said Dad. But, just as I turned to get into the car, the rain stopped and a beam of sunlight broke through the dark clouds. A man came out of the house and asked in English if he could help us. The church bells in the village started to ring and I heard ducks quacking loudly close by. I didn't know it then, but it was the sound of fate.

The Englishman told us that the house was his daughter's and he was there to check it wasn't leaking too much. He invited us in for a cup of tea and to look around what was essentially a shell of a house. The wind howled through holes in the bare concrete walls and roof, and the floors had a strange tackiness to them. The house was dank, cold and smelled stale. The 'bathroom' was nothing more than a filthy shower cubicle on the hall landing, and the loo was in a corner of the kitchen. 'This house is not fit to live in,' Dad declared as he pulled at a bit of rotting wood on the kitchen doorframe.

But, as I peered out of the kitchen window that looked over a huge garden with wild birds flitting about, I saw fields beyond that stretched out as far as the eye could see and a church spire in the distance. I felt a pull on my heart strings. I had a vision of myself growing vegetables and fruit. I could see beyond the ugly rooms to admire the beautiful old oak beams that held up the ceilings and the ancient flintstone wall that ran across one of the downstairs rooms.

I realized that I'd been hit by what the French call a *coup de foudre* – a lightning bolt, or love at first sight. I could feel my heart beating wildly. I just knew that this neglected old dump had huge potential and was waiting for the right family to come along and bring it back to life. I also knew, then and there, that the family would be me and Mark. I went home in a daze.

Mark was unsure about taking on such a huge project, and we discussed for hours what it would mean to buy the house and whether we could really afford it. As we talked more about the building's potential and what we could do to restore it, Mark's builder instincts kicked in. A week later we put in an offer and it was accepted.

We sold Mark's beloved Jaguar to pay the deposit, and adjusted to a reality of no holidays or treats while we poured everything into a fund for the necessary building work and repairs. Four months after we first set eyes on it, the French farmhouse was ours. And we have been renovating ever since.

Quite why I fell head over heels for a house with metal doors that flapped in the wind and rattling windows sometimes mystifies me. I'm not sure how I managed to block out the state of the building and focus on the fact that it had an acre of garden (admittedly unkempt and complete with a sheep). I'd watched those TV shows, the ones where they take a rundown old house and turn it into a beautiful and desirable home, but that sort of thing always felt like a distant dream and something I'd never do. But when I walked into the farmhouse that day, it just felt like I had been struck by fate, although sometimes, when we're up to our elbows cleaning out the septic tank or mending our roof for the umpteenth time, it feels more like we might have been struck by something altogether less pleasant.

For almost ten years we spent most of our weekends and all of our holidays turning our hovel into a home. We explored the local area, met the neighbours and fell under the spell of a tranquil way of life until we were so in love with the village, the amazing street markets, the delicious French cakes and the friendly locals, that we could hardly bear to leave at the end of our visits.

We felt more and more torn between our lives in London and our feelings about this wonderful corner of France. I was about to be appointed as a director at the bank where I worked – it had taken eighteen years of hard slog to get there and I knew I deserved it. I loved my job and I felt far too young to retire. My dad said I was an idiot to even consider giving it all up. But I knew Mark was sick of never seeing me because of the long hours I worked during the week and sometimes at weekends, too.

When his beloved younger sister passed away from cancer, the loss hit him hard. She loved spending time with us in France and often talked about wanting to buy a house in the village. For Mark, being able to spend time with the people you love became more important than anything and he knew that we could make a different life in France together. In all honesty, it was a tough decision. I am not comfortable with risk. But I do believe in fate and love. There were obstacles along the way – at work there was a big project to which I was committed, and then Dad got diagnosed with cancer. I was devastated and I knew I couldn't abandon him when he needed me most. I went back and forth between France and the UK for two years, going to appointments, sitting with him through treatments, or just being there to make a cup of tea and listen when he wanted to talk. His death was a huge blow and left me reeling for a long time afterwards. But the words he'd said to me a thousand times echoed in my head: 'Life is for living. Don't waste one single precious moment.' And, so, one warm September day, almost ten years after we had been so sure we would never want to buy a house in France, we piled our belongings into a trailer and drove them to a little rural French village to begin a new life.

This is the tale of one year in France, a romp through the four seasons in the lives of two frequently baffled but determined expat Brits.

Janine Marsh

Oh, Là Là Land

ON THE FIRST day of the new year a heavy, freezing fog descended on the village and decided it was going to stay. The air hung, silent and cold, blanketing the houses and making the smoke from the chimneys hover over the rooftops in the absence of a breeze. Nothing much moved, except for a few hardy farmers taking food to cows hiding in warm barns and some hungry chaffinches looking for berries in the hedgerows. The houses had their shutters closed tight against the chill. Except for a few short hours when they were swung open to let in the day, they would remain like this throughout January, preserving the warmth from the wood fires and creating a semi-twilight world for those inside. It has been this way for centuries in the Seven Valleys. That was fine by me. I wasn't going anywhere after a New Year's Eve dinner the night before at the home of our neighbours Guillaume and Constance. We had feasted like kings and drunk like lords, and moving much today was out of the question.

At 8 p.m. the night before, a customary thirty minutes later than the time we were asked to arrive, Mark and I had set off from our house halfway up a hill in the middle of the lush Seven Valleys, rural northern France. It's been almost fifteen years since we – the only Brits in the village – bought our ramshackle old farmhouse, so we knew perfectly well that arriving later than asked is an unspoken law. Nobody seems to have a clue why this is so, and I have had many discussions with my French friends about how much easier it would be if they could just tell us what time they really want people to arrive. 'But this is how we've always done it,' they say. 'Our parents did it this way and their parents before them.' And, as everyone knows, in France, if it has always been that way, then it will stay that way whether it makes sense or not.

A five-minute walk down a country lane and alongside fields encircled by frost-kissed hedges brought us to our friends' home, a fortified, stone-built farmhouse typical of the area. We pushed open the gate, which squealed loudly in protest, making dogs howl and an owl hoot somewhere above our heads. Other than that, it was silent and pitch-black. We made our way to the front door via a slippery cobbled path and pulled a long chain, which set off a ringing that we could hear faintly through the heavy wooden door.

Ushered into a wood-fire-warmed dining room, we were somehow still the first to arrive, but at least we weren't too early. There had been occasions in the past when, not knowing the drill, we had turned up at the right time to find the hosts not even dressed. Thankfully the rest of the guests, all of whom we knew, arrived just minutes after. Jean-Claude and his wife Bernadette are (whisper it) our favourites. They welcomed us to the village from day one and Jean-Claude, especially, became our mentor and, at times, saviour. He frequently visits us, offering advice and explaining how things work around here. It was Jean-Claude who came to the rescue when we ran out of firewood in our first winter, apparently the coldest in years, and I was considering divorcing Mark due to the fact that it was his fault. I felt as if I was slowly freezing to oblivion because he had persuaded me that coming to France to live permanently was a good idea. Pushing back the flat cap that might just be glued to his head as I've never seen him not wearing it, Jean-Claude had pursed his lips while thinking about who might have wood for sale in winter and then ordered it for us. He told us where the best boulangeries were, the best time to plant potatoes, how to cut hedges properly and how to make crow pâté, which to tell the truth is not something I wanted to learn and can't honestly recommend.

Constance and Guillaume, who during the week live and work in the city of Lille, the capital of the region, inherited their village house. They love to cook and to teach me about French cuisine. We became good friends after we met at a party where everyone was required to make and bring a tart to be judged. That is considered fun in these parts, unless you are called 'flop chef, not top chef', as I am. Constance had baked a strawberry tart that everyone agreed was the best they had ever tasted. Delicate, light golden pastry, creamy and sweet crème pâtissière topped with strawberries macerated in Grand Marnier and dusted with icing sugar – it was heaven on a plate. She won first prize. I had made a rather sad cheese tart that no one had wanted to eat, and came last, which was not in the least bit surprising. Constance offered to teach me how to cook, and despite several people in the village over the years already trying and failing, I can now create a passable tart thanks to her gentle patience and encouragement.

Madame Bernadette (always called Madame Bernadette so as not to be confused with Bernadette, wife of Jean-Claude), a white-haired widow who lives alone in the corner house at the bottom of our hill, was sitting at the table. Next to her was old Monsieur Martel, who also lives alone. Both in their seventies, they have lived in the village and known each other all their lives, and bicker as if they were married. Jean-Claude, who is a terrible gossip, says that there has never been a romance between them and there is hardly likely to be as Monsieur Martel is a little rustic in his ways, whereas Madame Bernadette loves art and classical music. He keeps pigs, goats and ornamental chickens, and she has reproduction Monet paintings all over the house. According to Jean-Claude, this is the sort of clash that can't be overcome even though I've told him that he might be wrong. I had read that Monet apparently loved chickens. In fact, he was fanatical about them.

The final guests to arrive were Paul, who is Constance's cousin, and his partner Delphine. Paul is a maths teacher and sports a permanent hangdog expression, which gives the impression he might be quite sensible, whereas he is quite bonkers. He once had to choose between his beloved pet chicken Cherie, which lived permanently in his house and accompanied him in the car when he went to the shops, and nubile girlfriend of the time Sylvie, who refused to share a pillow with poultry. He chose Sylvie – he's not that bonkers – but the relationship was never quite the same. Paul pined for Cherie for months until Sylvie lost her temper and dumped him for a baker from Béthune. Delphine, with her calm and placid nature, is perfect for Paul. They bonded, she says, after meeting at a flea market and spotting at the same time a book about mushrooms that they both wanted, revealing their shared love of mushroom foraging. She allowed Paul to buy the book and he took her to a secret forest to find fungi. One fungi led to another and their wedding was planned for October.

Constance and Guillaume brought out little canapés: tarts with baked eggs and truffle shavings, blinis with grilled herring, jellied vegetables and slices of dried sausage that were perfect with the chilled champagne. After that it was on to entrées, starting with snails swimming in lurid green garlic butter so hot it was bubbling, and fresh oysters from Boulogne-sur-Mer less than an hour away. When we sat down to the main course, Guillaume carried in a huge tureen of stew called beef carbonnade, cooked with beer and brown sugar – everyone cheered as he whipped off the lid and aromatic steam filled the room. Each course was accompanied with a wine perfectly paired with the dish.

Just before 12 p.m., Guillaume counted '*dix, neuf, huit, sept, six, cinque, quatre, trois, deux, un* …', and we all kissed on the cheeks and wished each other *bonne année*. Mark and I hugged each other tight, but not anyone else in the room – the French don't hug, they kiss. If I had tried to hug one of our hosts or their guests, it's almost certain that a rumour would have started circulating about the weird British woman being a hugger. It's bad enough that I'm known to some people as Madame Merde after my septic tank exploded.

Then it was time for the cheese, served before dessert in France. It was a beautiful display from the famous Fromagerie Caseus in nearby Montreuil-sur-Mer. A cheese course in France isn't just a stage in the meal – it's a history lesson on a plate. Local cheeses in these parts that are firm favourites include Mimolette, Maroilles and Vieux Boulogne. Aged Mimolette, which originates in Lille and has a right royal history, is considered to be best. When France fell out with Holland in the seventeenth century, Louis XIV banned the import of Edam cheese and commanded that a French equivalent be made – only better. Local cheesemakers in Lille, tasked with this tall order, came up with a ball-shaped cheese with an orange rind. They also discovered they could add extra flavour by introducing cheese mites to the surface, where they dig little holes. It doesn't look or taste similar to Edam but it stayed because everyone liked it so much! Except in America, where it's banned because of the bugs.

Maroilles is incredibly smelly but delicious and was invented by monks in the town of Maroilles more than a thousand years ago. And Vieux Boulogne, which despite its name is quite a new cheese, invented in 1982, is officially the stinkiest (or most fragrant, if you're French) cheese in the world according to scientists at a university in the UK. Thankfully there was no Gris de Lille, which the locals call 'stinky grey' or the 'stench of Lille'. Believe me, if you are ever unlucky enough to have some in your mouth, you will probably call it many names worse than that (although apparently the Soviet leader Nikita Khrushchev fell head over heels for it when he visited Lille in 1960, and had a load shipped to Moscow). It doesn't actually come from Lille, but from Hainaut, near the border with Belgium, but when it was first made in the nineteenth century, it was sent to Lille to be preserved, developed and packed, hence the name. Let's just say that if you like the aroma of old and sweaty socks, you'll love the stinky grey.

We discussed new year's resolutions over the cheese course. This being France, there is a distinctly philosophical air to many discussions. Whether your aim is to get fitter, as many of us announced, or you want to learn to speak another language, which no one announced, you must talk about it as much as you can. The French absolutely love to have long, complicated discussions, to introduce topics into the conversation that will have no conclusion, to never admit to being wrong and to never say they don't know the answer to a question.

Madame Bernadette surprised no one when she announced that this year's goal was exactly the same as last year's. And the year before. Rumour has it that she has been on a diet since 1972. Sometimes it's tough living here in the rural north of France. We're surrounded by little villages with tempting boulangeries and pâtisseries, and I guarantee that the aroma of fresh-baked baguettes from a wood oven, lifted out by a ruddy-faced baker on the end of a long paddle, or the scent of flaky, buttery and golden just-cooked croissants, is utterly irresistible.

And then there are the cakes. Cake makers in France are craftsmen. They train for years learning how to make perfect little edible works of art. Opera cakes, Paris-Brest, eclairs, macarons – classic French cakes really are in a league of their own.

Regions, departments and even some towns have pastry specialities that are unique to them. Here in the far north, the *merveilleux* (marvellous) is a favourite. A speciality from Lille, it's a seriously sweet meringue puffball of a cake covered with whipped cream, chocolate or other sweet things. I can promise you, it requires fortitude to eat a whole one.

In the little town of Beaurainville, the local baker makes a cake that I've never seen anywhere else, though I am not sure you could put it in the category of great French gateaux. *Le doigt de Charles Quint* is a long sponge finger – literally. Red jam and Chantilly cream ooze from the centre. It's meant to represent the gouty pinky finger of Emperor Charles V who once ruled these parts. It tastes better than it sounds ... There are even seasonal cakes and breads. A *galette des rois* (kings' cake) is de rigueur in January, as are *bûches de Noël* (yule log) in December and cherry clafoutis in spring.

I am always reading in some newspaper or other that French women are somehow able to exert superhuman strength over their appetites and remain skinny. That might be true in Paris where, at the posh Café de la Paix next to the Opéra de Paris, I once saw a pencil-thin woman order a bowl of lettuce for dinner as her lover (I knew because they were kissing each other with wild abandon and much flashing of tongues across the table in between mouthfuls) tucked into succulent oysters, a juicy steak and ended with a dreamy tarte Tatin. But I promise you, your average French woman, at least where I live, is quite normal and able to resist anything but temptation – just like the rest of us.

Madame Bernadette *loves* cakes. The Bread Man (not a man made of bread but the man who delivers bread and pastries to our village, and many others around, three times a week) knows this, and he is a good salesman. In January, he hardly mentions the sweet feasts he has in the back of his van. The dieting Madame Bernadette accepts her lonely baguette with a sigh. By February, she will be asking 'Do you have a mille-feuille?' By March, the Bread Man is openly tempting her with sugar cakes (a sweet pastry baked with a thick butter and sugar topping), pastel-pink macarons, passionfruit pavlovas or a sticky and creamy coffee religieuse. The battle is lost. Resistance is futile. But as Madame Bernadette says, there's always next year …

Around 1 a.m. Constance brought out cakes that looked like works of art. They were from Patrick Hermand in Le Touquet, which, if you're ever in the town, you can spot by the queue of people drooling at the window over the magical display.

By now, much as I love cake, I was thinking that Mark might have to roll me home in a wheelbarrow. I was aching from laughing as we played charades, the game where you have to act out a word or phrase without talking and everyone has to guess it. But this being France, there were rules that were different from wherever else you might play it. Everyone had to act out being a celebrity. Added to that there was a strict time limit. You had two minutes to present your charade and the guests had five minutes to discuss and guess. Jean-Claude, Paul and Monsieur Martel were all the late, great Johnny Hallyday, the French Elvis Presley. And believe me, the sight of more than one rather drunken, elderly Frenchman gyrating his hips to the imaginary sound of French rock and roll in a small salon in middle-of-nowhere France is enough to give you nightmares. Then Madame Bernadette and Bernadette were both Edith Piaf, hunched over an imaginary microphone, shaking with passion, throwing arms wide and mouths wide open in full silent song. '*Non, non, non,*' said Constance, admitting she was miffed as she too wanted to be Edith Piaf, 'we must all be someone different.' The rules were changed. You had to mime being a celebrity who wasn't Johnny Hallyday or Edith Piaf.

Nobody could guess that Guillaume was Jacques Cousteau, the great sea explorer, as he lay on the floor, his long, thin frame face down, a thumb in his mouth and a finger pointed straight up (evidently this was meant to be a snorkel), with his other arm miming a diving position. And in my wildest dreams I would never, ever have figured out that Delphine's imaginary hair tossing and pouting lips was meant to be Brigitte Bardot. Nobody guessed that I was Joan of Arc, riding an imaginary horse and wielding an imaginary sword, but I was disqualified on the grounds that she was not a celebrity but a saint. Mark was Quasimodo, which everybody guessed.

Some hours later, I could swear I heard a cockerel crowing outside and I noticed everyone was by now openly yawning. I've found that French people are terrible at ending a get-together. Whether it's an artisan who's come in for a cup of coffee at the end of a job, a neighbour who has popped in to borrow a packet of sugar, or a party, no one ever wants to be first to say goodbye. Being British, though, we're very good at calling it a day, and announced that we needed to go home. We said goodnight and good morning, kissed everyone again, and pulled on our coats and hats. Immediately there was a rush by everyone else to join us. A straggle of tired and tipsy villagers made their way home, pushing through the frozen air blanketing the silent village, crossing fields, along muddy alleyways and onto the silent main road.

It felt like I'd been asleep for five minutes when my alarm went off. There was no chance for a lie-in with animals to feed. My first job was to visit the bird pens, where my ducks, chickens and geese weren't remotely grateful or sympathetic to my fatigue and honked, clucked and quacked loudly for their own feast. Then the cats needed feeding and cuddles, the dogs needed walking and the fire needed stoking. And finally, it being New Year's Day after an all-night eat-athon, we could 'relax'. That meant we got back to the job of tiling the kitchen floor.

With twenty-one rooms to renovate, we had started with laying concrete floors inside the house and some hard standing outside so cars would not get stuck in the mud –

it rains a lot here. Over the years, Mark estimates, we've laid more than a hundred tons of concrete.

Then, we'd replaced all the old wood-framed windows with double-glazed PVC. It wasn't what I wanted – I had dreamed of lovely bespoke wooden windows – but we had thirty-seven windows to fit and the cost of the wooden ones would have bled us dry. And, in such a damp part of France, we would have needed to paint them every year. So, in the end, and after much heated debate, I caved in to the sensible option.

After that, we moved on to insulating the house, boarding the walls and ceilings, and plastering. Then everything had to be painted and cupboards built, electrics installed, sinks, showers and loos fitted. Tiling the kitchen floor was the last job we had to do before that room and the adjoining walk-in pantry were finished, and we were determined that, despite my dad's prediction that this house would be a never-ending job, we would finish the entire renovation by the end of this year.

Tiling isn't just tiling in this part of France. It's not just a question of nipping to the local hardware or tile shop to choose your tiles and take them home in the boot of the car. We have to drive for an hour to get to a store with a greater choice than just plain beige squares, which are a firm favourite in these parts. In the week before

Christmas we hitched up the trailer to the car, headed to Boulogne-sur-Mer on the Opal Coast and the Brico Depot superstore, where they know us by sight because of the amount of time we spend there buying materials. By the end of January, all the tiles were to be laid and everything in the kitchen ready to go. It would soon be our turn to host a dinner for our neighbours!

The cold fog lingered for several days. The water in the dogs' bowls iced over within an hour of being filled, and the pond in the ducks' pen was solid. Everything liquid turned to ice and every day I had to carry buckets of water down to the bird pens. The cats decided to hibernate in the house. Even Winston, who's known as the biggest cat in the village, came in to sleep at night, a rare occurrence these days. When I first found him under the wheels of our van in Boulogne, a tiny, bleeding bundle of fur with bright blue eyes (he'd been attacked by a bigger cat), I was totally smitten with what was my first pet. I nursed him back to health, feeding him kitten milk with a pipette until he was well enough to eat on his own.

Winston was a bit mad right from the start. If the doorbell rings, he hides. If someone comes into the house that is not me or Mark, he hides. Over the years he has gradually become more and more of a loner, disappearing sometimes for days on end. He comes in for food as long as there is no music, no strangers are present and the chairs in front of the door are in the same place – he really doesn't like change.

During the cold evenings, he lies watching the flames dance while he stretches out on a cushion with lazy Loulou the tortoiseshell cat, 'Enry Cooper, a fluffy feline with Zorro-mask-like eyes, and Shadow the black cat.

Ella Fitzgerald, who was supposed to be a spaniel but turned into a rather large German shepherd who doesn't think she is a dog at all, likes to lie on her own cushion. Bruno the Labrador lies across my feet, and Churchill the German pinscher (like a miniature Dobermann, but yappy) joins the cats in front of the fire where it's warmest.

The only cat who wasn't there in the cold spell was Hank Marvin He's Always Starvin', the one-eyed cat. He was in another room as his incurable cat flu made him sneeze constantly, so he had an enclosed cage that was easy to clean (one of my least favourite jobs). He cast broken-hearted looks at me when I carried him through the house and he saw the others living it up in the front room by the fire, but the alternative was full-time cleaning of cat snot off every surface. There are times when I look at what has become of my life and I shake my head in bewilderment.

Even now, years after we fitted the wood fire, I appreciate it more than I ever thought possible. Like many old houses in these parts we don't have central heating and rely on a single fire to keep the whole house warm. Often people around here grow their own trees and chop their own wood. Communal land is also used to grow trees for wood and the mayor allocates parcels to people in the village to use for their wood needs – always a great opportunity for manly wood-chopping get-togethers.

By Saturday night, a few days after New Year's Eve, we needed a break from the tiling and felt lively enough to venture out to Arnaud's bar in a town nearby. There are no shops, bars or cafés in our village. There is a main street and a few side streets, around 100 houses, a town hall, an old church, 142 people and 1,000 cows. But there are several towns not far away with bars and cafés, supermarkets, cheese shops, chocolate shops and boulangeries, and everything we need to live life to the full in the French way.

Although most people had by now taken down their Christmas decorations, we were surprised to find that Arnaud's was looking mind-bogglingly festive – unusual in itself for rural France but even more so since he is known to be a man who is not prone to wanton spending. He is said to enjoy counting his centimes fondly. Normally the bar is a rather minimalist place with dim lights, dark wooden tables and chairs spread through two large rooms of a house. You can peep through the curtains behind the bar and see the family kitchen, and regulars like to play 'What is Arnaud having for dinner today?' as the smell from the cooking pots wafts through to the bar. The dark wooden counter, with its floral porcelain pumps for the obligatory Leffe and Stella Artois beers, is always propped up by elderly farmers in their uniform of blue, green or brown boiler suits, sipping a glass of strong red wine or a throat-burning nip of Calvados, an apple brandy from neighbouring Normandy. There are black-and-white photos of unknown vintage boxers on the walls. It's said that Madame Armandine, Arnaud's mother, has never explained who the pictures are of, but it's thought that one of them might be a long-lost love. There's not a lot to do in these parts so imaginations tend to run wild. There is no basis for the story other than someone once suggested it thirty years ago. What is true is that Madame Armandine has a goal in life. She recently read about a barmaid in a town not far from here who, at one hundred years old, is the oldest barmaid in France. Now Madame is going all out to match or beat the record. Since the time taken to pour a beer is already painfully long, we are all going to suffer through this ambition with her – for the next seventeen years.

When I say that the bar looked as if the love child of Liberace and Andy Warhol had run amok with reels of tinsel, spray cans of glitter, fake snow and shiny paper chains, while under the influence of mind-altering drugs, that is an understatement. Everyone who came through the door let out an '*Oh, là là.*' Not so much *La La Land* as *Oh, Là Là Land*.

'*C'est psychédélique,*' said Monsieur Martinez, one of the regulars, as we looked around in wonderment at the radiant cave that the normally dour bar had become, wondering if we were hallucinating.

The reasons for this unusual festive spending soon became clear. 'We're closing at seven-thirty tonight,' said Arnaud as he poured our drinks, 'for *maman*'s birthday.' He nodded at the old lady who was sitting in the corner knitting a coat for her giant dog, a hairy white Pyrenean mountain dog that's bigger than her. When she takes it for a walk everyone stops to smile as it's the size of a small pony and she is the size of a hobbit. Fortunately for her, the dog has a good nature and is very lazy, or it could certainly take her for a walk.

We joined Monsieur Martinez at a table of regulars who were openly discussing the new-look bar. 'Arnaud's trying to show his new girlfriend he's not a meanie with the money,' said one. 'It won't last, remember that time ...' said another and they all raised their eyebrows. 'What time?' I whispered so that Arnaud wouldn't hear.

Monsieur Martinez, a former postman with a penchant for storytelling, picked up his Picon beer (a beer with a shot of orange liqueur) and settled back in his chair. 'Many years ago,' he began, 'Arnaud was in love with a woman who made cheese in Azincourt. Besotted with her, he was. Wanted to marry her and spend the rest of his life with her.' He stopped and took another sip of his beer. 'But they had a big falling-out because of his penny-pinching. He's always been that way, but his girlfriend couldn't live with it. She wanted her hair done and he arranged for his friend to do her hair as a surprise. But it was a disaster. The hairdresser cut off her long hair and put pink streaks in. And then when Arnaud said he didn't know what she was moaning about because it wasn't expensive, she dumped him.'

Everyone in the bar was of the opinion that for Arnaud to have spent money on such eye-popping decorations for the bar, which had been through many Christmases over the years without any change in décor whatsoever, it must be love.

'Who is the new girlfriend?' I asked. 'Is she local?'

'No,' said Monsieur Martinez. 'She works at the boulangerie on the corner.'

'I thought Berthe worked there,' I said. 'Has she left?'

'No, it's Berthe that he's going out with.'

'But surely she's local. She told me she only cycles for about fifteen minutes to get here.'

Monsieur Martinez arched his eyebrows. 'That's not local,' he said. 'Local is if you're born in the town.' Suddenly I remembered my neighbour Jean-Claude telling me his nickname, after forty-five years of living in our village, is still '*l'étranger*', even though he's from just 5 kilometres away.

Meanwhile the conversation in the bar was quite literally sparkling as everyone was covered in glitter, which sprinkled and swirled about every time the door was opened and the wind from outside took a turn around the room. Instead of putting glasses on top of coasters, we used coasters to try to keep the glitter out of our drinks. It was in my hair, in Monsieur Martinez's thick eyebrows and in Mark's beard.

When Arnaud announced it was time to close, everyone wished Madame Armandine a happy birthday and kissed her on the cheek, and we left them to their birthday dinner. As we drove home through the wiggly country lanes of the Seven Valleys, it looked as if the whole area had been abandoned. Shutters were closed tight against the cold and the wind, and we drove for miles without seeing a single human being. But, if you're ever in these parts on a winter's day, simply look up and you'll see wispy smoke cheerfully floating from chimneys. Inside the houses, life goes on, warm and cosy, centred on a wood fire or a coal oven – very useful in the countryside where stormy weather causes power cuts from time to time. When that happens, we rely on candlelight, read lots of books and try to stay calm, though it's not always easy when your job relies on the internet.

Back home, as I opened the door of the house, with the wood fire still glowing, I thought I could smell smoke from my dad's roll-up cigarettes in the air. There are times when his presence is so strong that I can almost believe he is still with us. It was several years after we bought the house as a holiday home, renovating at weekends and on holidays, that Mark persuaded me that it would be a good idea to give up our jobs in London and our comfy home in the suburbs to spend more time together and do up our French folly. It was going to be a temporary thing as we knew at least one of us would have to go back to London to earn money to live.

But it was just a few months into our new lives when my dad found out he had lung cancer and it was terminal. The doctors estimated he had two years left. I went back to London sooner than anticipated and spent the next two years shuttling between London and France, looking after dad and helping with the renovation back in France when I could.

Dad signed up for a programme to test a new treatment, even though he knew it wouldn't help him and would make him even more tired than the disease itself and the conventional treatment. Ten years after we'd lost Mum to cancer, he was still counting the days since she'd gone and he felt that if his participation in the tests meant one person had a better time than her, then it would be worth it. Some days it exhausted him. He would sleep for hours and I'd sit quietly, waiting for him to wake, to make him a cup of tea or something to eat, and to just be there. When Dad awoke, he'd ask me to read my stories about life in France that I'd been scribbling down while he slept. Not prone to praise, one day he said, 'You should write a book. You're quite good.'

When he died almost exactly two years after he was diagnosed, I was heartbroken. First Mum and then Dad to the same terrible disease. My dad may have always said, 'Life is for living. Don't waste one single precious moment,' but there are times after you lose someone that you really don't feel like making the most of things. You want to sit and remember, and some days you howl at the loss. But my dad's words stayed with me and I was determined to make him proud. I went back to France resolute that we would get the renovation finished one day. And I began to write in earnest.

My friends and family had been quite sure I'd never last in France. I'd worked in an office job since school, I am a Londoner born and bred, and I didn't like the smell of cow poo. In my office, they said my set-up in France was like *The Good Life* (*The Good Neighbours* in the US), a sitcom about a middle-aged man who reaches a milestone in his life and decides to make a change, giving up his job and persuading his wife to join him in a quest to live a more self-sufficient lifestyle.

After Dad died, Mark built me a website and I started blogging. I called my site 'The Good Life France'. I wrote about my daily life, the places I visited, the people I met – anything and everything to do with France. It started as a fun way to keep friends up to date with my new life and the enormous renovation job we'd taken on. When other people started to read it, I was thrilled. The blog grew and grew, and I just couldn't stop writing! And my audience grew and grew, too.

I started a Facebook community page and made new friends with people from all around the world who have a common love of all things French. Every weekend we'd share photos – it's become a tradition on my page now and thousands of people join in.

Within a couple of years, the blog was getting more than a million views a month. It led to companies wanting to advertise on the website. I was asked to write about France for newspapers, magazines and other websites. One day a publisher contacted me and asked if I'd be interested in writing a book about my journey from city slicker to out-and-out country bumpkin.

The blog has led to me travelling all over France and discovering more and more about my adopted country, it's history, secrets, culture, gastronomy, people and monuments. Mark, meanwhile, studied to become an expert on building websites and how they work. It turned out he was incredibly good at it. To our surprise, in the end we didn't have to go back to our jobs in London.

Nouveau city slickers

BY FEBRUARY THE freezing fog had cleared and snow had arrived. The soft flakes fell on our village, smothering everything and muffling the sound of the tractors ferrying food to animal barns around the valleys.

The dogs loved to play in the white powder that dusted the hills and paths. We had to keep a close eye on them on our walks as the rabbits, hares and pheasants that are so prolific in the countryside were much easier to see against a white background and Ella Fitzgerald loved to chase them.

Not everyone loves the snow here, though, especially the old folk. In winter more than ever they rely on mobile deliveries. Pas-de-Calais, with a population of 1.2 million, is one of the most densely populated, as well as largest, departments in France, even though it has no large cities. It contains 895 villages and hamlets scattered throughout the lush countryside and along the coast. Some *communes*, as they are called, have shops, bars and businesses, but many have nothing. There's very little public transport in rural areas, and often none at all. But, long before reducing your carbon footprint became something to aspire to, this little part of France decided that making many people drive to the shops is daft, so they bring the shops to each village. Goods cost a few centimes more than you would pay in the shops, but nobody minds that at all.

When it snows, everyone in the village rallies round to make sure neighbours, especially the elderly or vulnerable, are looked after. It's not unique to my village: it's a normal part of life throughout the Seven Valleys.

To walk the dogs each morning I don scarf, thick, padded man-sized gloves, army-style parka, thick socks, welly warmers, welly boots and sometimes, if it's still dark, a beanie hat with a torchlight sewn into the rim. When I think that not that long ago I'd be trotting over London Bridge with all the other city slickers, on my way to the office wearing a smart coat, stiletto-heeled boots and carrying a briefcase, I doubt anyone would recognize the half-yeti who now makes her way up and down hills with three excitable dogs.

Jean-Claude doesn't enjoy snow at all as it means he has to walk. One morning I could hear him huffing and puffing in the road outside my gate before I even opened it. Usually he drives his little white van the few hundred yards from his house at the bottom of our hill to his mother-in-law Claudette's house at the top. He has a fondness for beer, wine, cheese, cakes, duck à l'orange, snails, frogs legs, mashed potato, chocolate pudding and much more. It shows. He's not exactly keen on exercise of any sort. He does the very short trip several times a day, checking on Claudette first thing in the morning, stopping in for coffee and *pain perdu* (French toast) every couple of hours, joining her for lunch – despite being nearly ninety years old, she cooks him a three-course meal from fresh ingredients every day. In the evening, if his wife is still at work, he will pop in to see if anything is needed before Claudette goes to bed at precisely 7 p.m. Along with rising at 5 a.m. all year round, gardening and exercising daily – and drinking a glass of homemade cider for breakfast alongside a slice of pork belly – Claudette swears that ten hours sleep a night is the secret to living to a ripe old age.

'*Zut alors*,' I said to Jean-Claude as I opened the gate to say hello, 'isn't it cold?' Jean-Claude frowned at me because no one really says '*Zut alors*' in France.

'*Merde*, isn't it cold?' he corrected me. 'Look at that idiot Thierry up the top of the hill. He has decided today of all days is a good day to deliver wood to someone and now he has got his tractor stuck.' He rolled his eyes to emphasize his frustration.

Earlier the sound of an engine being revved loudly and persistently had echoed around the village, bouncing off the hills and trickling along the tops of the trees. To tell the truth, I thought the racket was probably Jean-Claude as he refuses to buy a new battery to replace the worn out one in his old tractor and usually bump-starts it on the hill. But now I could see that it was Thierry who was causing the rumpus. He had indeed loaded several tons of wood onto a trailer on the back of his tractor, and having slithered out of the entrance to his farm he had lost control on the icy road. He had skidded and was now wedged sideways after narrowly avoiding crashing through the very prickly hawthorn hedge that lined the garden of the house opposite.

'I suppose I shall have to go and sort it out,' said Jean-Claude, who is the self-appointed officer-of-sorting-things-out in the village. He stomped up the road (not easy when it's slippery), muttering curses under his breath. Reaching the hapless Thierry, he began shouting instructions: 'Back, forward, back, forward, back, forward, turn, back, forward, back, forward …' The tractor went hither and thither, and Thierry's face turned puce. Eventually the tractor was free of the gate and facing the right way down the hill. Thierry went trundling past, refusing to look in my direction. Jean-Claude watched with narrowed eyes like Clint Eastwood seeing off his foe, gave a Gallic shrug and turned to walk through Claudette's gate for his morning coffee, his day's work done.

A little while later, he was back, saying he had a favour to ask for Claudette. Mark and I followed him up the hill to Claudette's house, which, at around two hundred years old, is considered relatively modern in these parts, and into an outbuilding at the side that leads to a gloomy cellar.

The tiny, fit-for-a-hobbit door to the cellar was broken. Jean-Claude said it had been there since the house was built and 'had seen better days'. Seen better days? He wasn't kidding. It looked like it was made from wooden lace and held together with sticky tape. Barely hanging on to a rusty hinge, the handle was a piece of string, and the woodworm holes looked more like wood-snake holes (if there were such a thing).

'Do you think you could fix it up?' Jean-Claude asked Mark, who everyone knows is a whiz with woodwork. 'I think maybe we'd better just make a new one,' Mark replied.

'On no, there's no need for that,' said Jean-Claude. 'It just needs a little bit of patching up. *Belle-maman* is used to this door. She's been using it for nearly ninety years.'

'She likes to make sure she gets the most use out of things,' Jean-Claude once told us. She has taught me to use the corks from bottles as kindling for the wood fire and to repurpose empty plastic bottles into mole deterrents. Plonked on the end of a stick, they tremble in a breeze and the vibration apparently scares the bejeezus out of a mole. Does it work? Well, my garden is still full of molehills, but Claudette assures me it would be even worse without the plastic-bottle deterrents.

Mark said he would give the door repair a go, but he didn't look convinced. As a thank-you, Jean-Claude wanted to give us some carrots. That's how it works round here between neighbours and friends – no hourly rate, but a swap instead.

Jean-Claude took us down the cellar stairs. Quite how a ninety-year-old woman goes up and down those steep steps in such gloomy light is beyond me. Fit for a goat is all I will say. In the earth-smelling underground cave, there was a mound of potatoes piled up against a wall and wooden barrels lined another wall. There was also a huge, old pram, which looked mouldy, and a long wooden crate filled with sand. Jean-Claude plunged his hands into it and came up with an enormous carrot. He brushed off the sand and bit into the end. The cellar echoed to the sound of his crunching.

'*Magnifique*, very juicy – from the field next to the one where Thierry keeps his horses in the summer,' he announced. He pulled out a couple of dozen carrots for us to take home. They might have been down there in that dark, cold cellar for a few months, but those carrots tasted as fresh as the day they came out of the ground. I love this way of helping each other out in the country – it really brings people together.

Once, a woman who lives around the corner knocked on the door and asked if we could give her husband a lift to pick up his car. It had slid off the road in the snow several miles away. He'd had it towed to a garage and managed to get them to drop him off home. (Taxis are just not an option where we are – we once enquired how much it would cost to take a taxi into the town and back, about a thirty-five-minute round journey: 120 euros came the answer. 'For that,' said Mark, 'I'd expect a gold-plated limo.') We'd never met the woman before but had seen her waiting with her son outside the town hall for the school bus. Despite the skating-rink condition of the road that day, Mark agreed to take the husband to his car. Arriving at the garage, the man's car was not in a good state but he told Mark that the garage staff were robbers and wanted too much money to repair it. He tied the dangling bumper up with string and revved the engine before thanking Mark for his help and shooting out the garage door and down the road. Mark was convinced, as he set off slowly and carefully, that he would find the car in a ditch on the way home. Luckily, that wasn't the case and the woman came round a couple of days later with several jars of jam and a large sponge cake.

Mark took Claudette's old door into his workshop. It used to be a garage, but we converted it as it seemed more important that we had somewhere to keep tools and build things for the house when we can't work outside due to the weather. He plonked the door down on his workstation and set about repairing it. Mark made a wooden frame and inside it he fitted the remains of the rotten old door that apparently meant so much to Claudette. He made little wooden dowels to fill in the holes and patched the rest up with wood glue and shavings. Once he'd rubbed it down, I could hardly see where the cavities had been. Then he fitted a new handle to the wooden frame and varnished the whole thing.

'*Mon ami*, you are a genius, the Leonardo da Vinci of the wood shop,' announced Jean-Claude when Mark returned and fitted the old door. Claudette came to inspect the work. '*Très bien*,' she said beaming and, patting down her silver hair, beckoned us into her kitchen for a glass of wine and to tell us stories of the old days when the village was a thriving place with several cafés and twice as many inhabitants as there are today. Wearing a nylon housecoat over a dress to keep it clean – apparently she has never owned a pair of trousers in her life – she told us tales of the back-breaking work that the farm boys did, how no one really went further than a couple of miles by horse and cart, and how it wasn't until 1940 that she saw a car for the first time.

'So much has changed,' she said wistfully, looking at us over the top of her little round glasses. She doesn't have a computer or a mobile phone, and has never used the internet. She has never been on a train, let alone an aeroplane, and has never visited Paris. She doesn't like it when I say, 'Have you never been ... never done ... or never seen ...?' She tells me I should focus on what has been done and seen. 'Life isn't always about what you have, what you can get, what you see and do. It's about family, friends and home. Those are the really important things and they are here, all around me. I don't have to go anywhere else to make me happy.'

Claudette spends most of her time in the kitchen where she has an old television that sits on top of her ancient fridge and shows images in black and white. Her enamel-embossed oven is more than sixty years old, a wedding present, though sadly her husband has long since passed.

when he and his ancient wife come out with their long sticks to keep the cows on track to cross the road. Cars stop on either side of the line of slow-moving, mooing cows. Mr and Mrs Vache, as we call them, keep the huge animals on track from one field to another, though the cows are curious creatures and would lick the cars and stick their heads into open windows to have a good look at the creatures inside if they were allowed. The traffic jams only occur when the weather is good. In the winter, the cows stay in their barns, snug and warm with hay bales to munch on to keep them going through to spring.

The bitterly cold February weather meant that extra vigilance was needed in the garden when it came to my pet chickens, ducks and geese. They're always excited to see me but on very chilly days they are really quite joyful when I open the door of the kitchen at the back of the house and they see I'm about to take care of them. A cacophony of clucks, quacks and honks fills the garden, prompting the wild birds to stop pecking at the fat balls and seeds I put out for them and look around to see what all the fuss is about. I do all the usual things, such as making sure there's plenty of dry straw in the coops and ferrying buckets of water from the house when their troughs and ponds freeze. Some days, when I feel really sorry for them, I'll make them some rice or porridge and serve it slightly warm.

A man in Arnaud's bar once told me that it was important to make sure each bird is mobile, as when temperatures are so cold it's not unusual for a bird to find its feet completely frozen to the ground. Of course, I knew this couldn't possibly be true, but I asked Madame Bernadette, who's an experience poultry keeper, just to be sure.

'Absolutely true. I've had to chisel a duck out of the icy mud many a time,' she assured me with a serious face.

'Surely not,' I said. 'That must be a joke?'

'*Non*,' she said firmly. 'It happens. You must check that none of your birds get stuck in the ice. It can cause serious injury and even death.'

I told Mark what Madame Bernadette had said. 'Surely not,' he also said. 'That must be a joke.'

As neither of us were completely certain, we took some old wooden pallets down to the pens to give the birds somewhere to keep off the frozen ground. Every day I checked but never saw any signs of this apocalyptic prediction coming true. The birds loved jumping on and off the pallets, though, and playing chick-king of the castle!

Chickenitis, as my friends call it, has crept up slowly on me since the move to France. In their opinion, I have become addicted to keeping chickens as pets. But there's something very soothing about spending time with these feathered creatures – despite living in this wonderfully tranquil countryside, my life is quite frenetic at times. You might think that, if anything, a flock of fifty birds, a mix of chickens, ducks and geese, would simply add more stress. But I assure you it has the opposite effect.

When I'm frazzled, taking five minutes out to sit in the pen and watch my birds live their lives is very calming. They boss each other about, inspect everything that moves and chase the wild birds off their food. There are wrens, chaffinches, tits, pigeons, woodpeckers, robins, jays, magpies and even pheasants – but it's the doves that really get everyone going.

The ducks are very offended at the dove intruders and race around flapping their wings. The geese waddle furiously, honking loudly. The chickens seem to take a deep breath, hitch up their skirts, figuratively speaking, and dash over to have a look. There is always one chicken, usually Joan Crawford, the bossiest and meanest of them, that puts on a spurt and sprints across the pen. Of course, the doves always escape. Dozens of them roost in the trees that surround the pens, waiting stealthily until the chicken ninjas' backs are turned, then they drop down to the food trays to start again.

I'm always amazed at the difference in chicken personalities. In one pen, the girls are very house-proud, their coop always quite clean. The pen next door, on the other hand, is completely different. They trash it and sit back to wait for the maid to clear up after them. The good girls wander around while I clean, inspecting the newspapers I use to line their trays and the straw that goes in the nest boxes. The bad girls, led by Joan Crawford, want to get involved. The little gang of black and white birds, some fluffy-footed, others bouffant-haired, are poultry hooligans who jump up into the coop while I'm cleaning, rooting around and clucking loudly with a protesting tone. They climb into the bucket where I put their waste to go to the compost heap. They shred the newspapers that line the coop, pull the straw out, and the minute I'm done there's a race up the ladder to be the first in and leave their mark. At least that's how it seems.

Meanwhile, having completed the tiling of the kitchen floor and the finishing touches in January, the last room in the house to be renovated was finally ready to use. We'd started with a long narrow room with walls, painted a very lurid yellow (apparently inspired by Monet's kitchen at Giverny in Normandy), that frequently ran with condensation, the water pooling in a dip in the floor. In one corner there had been a very old loo (yes, in the kitchen), though it was roughly boxed off with thin plywood. There was also a chipped china sink in another corner, opposite a coal-fired oven of indeterminate age that started billowing smoke when we tried to light it. There were a few rotting old cupboards with plenty of rat and mouse droppings in them, and a few mismatched worksurfaces. For years we cooked on a barbecue in the garden.

Over time we added a small extension to create space for a table and chairs overlooking our acre of garden. We fitted wide lantern lights, bought cheap on eBay – horribly heavy and hard to fit – to the roof of the extension to let in more light. We bought cheap cupboard carcasses from a DIY store and then made our own doors and worktops. We installed a new sink and a range oven that works on bottled gas as we have no gas mains. We covered up the well hole in the middle of the room (no one wants to fall down that in the middle of dinner) and built a walk-in pantry with cupboards made of the wood from our old staircase. I would like to tell you it was enjoyable doing up the kitchen but there were times when I could have easily just given up. Twice the pipes burst when the temperature dropped well below freezing, despite copious amounts of protective insulation. The kitchen and extension were flooded both times. The kitchen was the room in the house that took the longest to do, with lots of electrical wiring, plug sockets and lights, the removal of the disgusting loo and new plumbing to fit. As we have a septic tank rather than mains drains, doing that wasn't half as much fun as you might think.

We studied YouTube tutorials on fitting kitchens, scoured design magazines and the internet for ideas, and took our time to get it right. When we finished it was with great relief and enormous joy that we popped open a bottle of champagne and celebrated having a real kitchen, more than ten years after we'd bought the house. It might seem like a long time but in the village of Embry nearby, we knew a couple who had had no clean running water for the best part of twenty years. They didn't live in the house full time but took all their holidays there and would bring out copious amounts of cutlery, glasses and dishes, and wrap them all up in paper to take home to wash.

Now that it was completed, I decided that it was time to try out the kitchen. Thanks to Constance's cooking lessons and encouragement, I've improved considerably as a cook, but lack discipline. Mark, though not exactly chef of the year, is more focused than me and he doesn't have a social media account, which is my downfall. I love chatting on Facebook, Twitter and Instagram. I read every comment someone puts on a photo or post that I share, and reply to as many as I can, and sometimes there are hundreds of comments. And I answer every question someone posts, and there are sometimes a great deal of them. I start out with good intentions when cooking, but often simply get caught up chatting. Frequently I'm alerted by the smoke alarm going off, which Mark now calls the timer.

So, though Mark normally cooks, I thought I would surprise him by making some cupcakes. When I presented them to him, they looked a bit brown (sort of mahogany coloured). 'I'm sorry,' I confessed, 'but someone asked me on Facebook about where the best place for hot chocolate was in Paris, and by the time I finished telling them I was a little late getting them out of the oven.' Mark managed to ignore the charred tops and bit into one. They were apparently very good – for building walls. Generally the animals love what I cook. They don't seem to mind my slightly blackened and wizened offerings.

That month we lost Hank Marvin He's Always Starvin', the cat who liked my cooking the most. His flu got worse over the winter and, despite injections from the vet, one night he just went to sleep and didn't wake up. I was utterly heartbroken to lose this poor little cat. I'd only had him for eighteen months, since the day he'd turned up at the back door on my birthday, his eyes horribly red with a raging infection. He was so skinny it made me cry to see his bones stick out. It took me weeks to get him to trust me, leaving food for him in the garden every day. But one day, after he had bitten me so hard that his needle-sharp teeth pierced my fingernail and I still persisted, he decided I was going to be his mum. I rushed him to the patient vet in the town of Hucqueliers, who managed to save one of Hank's eyes, and I managed to get the cat to eat. Hank, or Skank as everyone else called him, put on weight and followed me everywhere. He loved cuddles, so to hold him I would put on a long-sleeved housecoat to cope with his constant sneezing, which would be interspersed with very loud purring. But he was never a well cat. We buried him near the chicken coop where he loved to sit and watch the birds play, never chasing them.

It wasn't long before another cat turned up. I think there is a sort of feline grapevine in our village and the word went around that there was a vacancy at the house of the animal-mad British woman. In addition to my own cats, I feed a number of waifs and strays. The people across the road moved out just after Christmas and left their two cats behind, so I put food out for them too and left the door of the woodshed open so they would have shelter.

The new cat, however, was clearly not like the others: she was hugely padded and not at all feral. She had a pretty but grumpy face and meowed frequently. We called her Fat Cat. We were sure she had been well looked after but no one in the village knew of her. We took her to the vets to see if she was chipped. 'She's not a biter like those other strays you bring in, is she?' said the vet, eyeing Fat Cat suspiciously. I assured him she was tame and sweet-natured. Apparently she had a cold and the vet gave her some medicine – also informing us that she was in fact a he!

'Ow many cats is zis? FIVE? You Brits,' he said, 'you are all ze same. Cats, dogs, 'orses and goats … first one, then another until you are almost a zoo.' Ah well, I always tell him, there are worse things, eh?

And so the hole in our hearts left by Hank Marvin was filled with an enormous, fluffy cat who doesn't like to move and has a gargantuan appetite. The name Fat Cat stuck. Luckily the other cats took to him and let him eat what he likes. He occasionally makes a feeble effort to join us for morning walks with the dogs, but has never made it further than the end of our fence.

Those morning walks take us through the village, past a little chapel big enough for half a dozen people, built by a local man in honour of his late wife. From there we head up into the hills and fields of the Seven Valleys. Every day I see the same people: Jean-Claude in his van, driving to the home of Claudette to check she's well; Bernadette on her way to her office job in town, leaving her husband free to find ways to spend the day avoiding things to do; Madame Bernadette cleaning the doorstep, dusting the walls or walking with her little shih-tzu that yaps incessantly and squares up to our dogs. Twice a week, I see the mayor's assistant, industriously typing away in the town hall. Then there's Jean-François, who cuts the village's hedges and grass, and keeps it looking spick and span; and the Young Man, who moved to the village in his early twenties.

At the top of the rue du Chapelle, there is a field with two very large pure white horses in it. They are Boulonnais horses, an ancient breed in the region going back to the first century when the Romans brought a similar breed of horse with them, and are owned by an old farmer who lives in the village. Every night we see him come by on his antiquated tractor with a small box with feed or hay on the back. In warm months he stops where the grass is long under the hedgerows and pulls out a rusty scythe. Despite his great age (well into his seventies) he swings at the grass, piling up the cuttings in the box. Traditional ways are held in high esteem around here.

As he approaches the field, the largest white horse hears the gentle putt-putt of the old tractor and races to the gate like a youngster, though she too is very old. She is a big, muscular horse and comes from a line of horses that were used to pull heavy carts, but she is very tender as she nuzzles the old farmer, snuffling softly and shaking her head. They clearly adore each other. The other white horse, her daughter, is more reticent and ambles over slowly, almost nonchalantly. Kids …

Sometimes there is a giant stork – pure white, too – in the field with the horses. It is almost magical when you see them all together. There are times when I pinch myself at how beautiful this place is and how very lucky I am to have had the chance to appreciate its gentle, authentic and seasonal beauty.

Everyone addresses the ancient farmer as 'monsieur'. Each night when I see him chatting away to his horses I call out '*Bonjour, Monsieur.*' Usually he waves and calls '*Bonjour*' before turning back to the horses and hay, to cleaning out their stable or filling their water butt, and off we both go about our business.

One day he introduced a young horse to the field, another pure white Boulonnais, a male this time. When we passed by, it galloped towards us to stick its big head over the hedge and neighed excitedly. We said hello and gave it some grass from the verge. When we left, it raced along the fence with my dogs and was generally very playful. One night, after I called out my customary *bonjour*, Monsieur called out to me as I walked on, 'What do you think of my new horse?' Surprised, I stopped and turned. 'Well,' I said, 'I think he's gorgeous. He's given a new lease of life to the older ones, hasn't he?' As I said this, the young one ran over and started chewing the old man's sleeve. The other two horses, including the one that is usually a bit stand-offish, also galloped over and were jealously vying for the old man's attention. 'Perhaps it's time for me to introduce someone younger into my life,' the old man said, laughing. He's been on his own, according to Jean-Claude, for more than thirty years. Then he winked at me. Since then, we've returned to our usual *bonjour* greetings, but every now and again he does stop and chat about the weather, his horses or the Parisians who have moved to our village.

At the end of last year, our Belgian neighbours moved about 2 kilometres down the road to an even smaller hamlet to live in a bigger house. They sold their old house to Parisians. This was big news in our village. Claudette, who at nearly ninety is not the oldest person in the village, has a very good memory and told us, 'The last time we had Parisians here was nearly fifty years ago. I remember it well. They wore high-heeled shoes and fur coats to walk their whiny little poodle around the village – the ladies that is, not the men.' She can still crack a joke despite her great age.

The last Parisians apparently lived in our house. During its four hundred or so years, the house has been an animal barn, a peasant dwelling, a café, the village telephone exchange and then, in 1971, the poodle-owning Parisians bought it. They left the enormous telephone exchange sign up in one of the rooms but built around it – it's still there and we too have built around it. One of these days, when we finally finish renovating, I'll get this old sign's light working.

The Parisians lined the walls with newspapers dating from May to October 1971. They are still there, hidden behind the new internal walls that we put up. I like to think that hundreds of years from now (when this old house will surely still be standing as Mark builds as if preparing for the apocalypse, with reinforced walls and floors) someone will find the newspapers on the wall and be amazed by them. The Parisians also put hideous pinewood panels everywhere, lining room after room with vile orange planks, sucking all the light and life out of the place. The panels are long gone now but the memory haunts me still. When we took them down, we discovered why they had done it. Previous, much earlier, owners, maybe as long as a hundred years ago or more, had smeared a mix of mud, dung and straw up to twelve inches thick across the walls and ceilings to act as insulation. I can't tell you how much fun it wasn't to dig it all out and get rid of several tons of decades-old animal poo.

No one has seen our new neighbours, so we don't know if they are wearing high-heeled shoes on our muddy, cow-trodden *rues*. Or if they have a poodle – as it is believed all

Parisians do. But their car has been spotted and apparently it is clean, which has amused everyone as no car stays clean around here. Someone has allegedly confirmed that lights are on in the house on some weekends (I am not quite sure how they know this as the Parisians have erected a tall wooden fence all the way round). Monsieur Partout, as he is known (it means Mr Everywhere and is the name given to a villager who likes to knows what's going on; there's one in every village), has on a daily basis been wandering down the little alleyway to the Parisians' house. As there is nothing else down there except an old footpath that leads to another tiny village a couple of miles away, he has only one reason to be there – spying and reporting back to the village grapevine.

It occurred to me that my neighbours must have been doing this when we first came here. They probably discussed what we wore and how strange and clueless we were. The fact that we are included in the gossip about the newcomers must mean that although we are still '*les étrangers*', the foreigners, we are accepted enough to be included in discussions about the nouveau city slickers.

I am still, even after a few years in France, in love with the fact that sometimes the most dramatic and newsworthy thing to happen in the village is the possibility of spotting inappropriately-dressed-for-middle-of-nowhere-rural-France-with-a-poodle-maybe city slickers from Paris.

Party like it's spring

THE HUNTING SEASON is a way of life in France. Whether you love it or hate it, that's how it is. We rarely walk the dogs at the weekends between September and March as that's when most hunting goes on, and being surrounded by the sound of the guns popping off isn't exactly relaxing. When we do go out, we see far less of the deer, rabbits, hares, pheasants and boars that are a common sight.

On the way home from a shopping expedition to Brico Depot to buy yet more building supplies (it's never-ending), Mark and I drove up and down the steep hills that run through the forests on the outskirts of the town. The woodland covers a huge area, with pine and oak trees towering above scrubland that is covered with wild garlic, bluebells and primroses in late spring. In early March, however, it's still largely leafless and you can clearly see animal paths running through the trees. We were chatting away about our next job when I spotted, just inside the bushes on the outskirts of the forest, a pair of wild pigs.

'Pull over slowly,' I said to Mark. 'I'll see if I can get a photo.'

As we stopped, I saw the pigs creep gingerly to the edge of the road, squealing and grunting, as their darting eyes, full of fear, stared at the cars whizzing by. I got out of the car and called, 'Hello pigs.' They stayed where they were, just a few feet away, staring at me. They were young pigs, bigger than a fully grown Labrador, with bristly brown hair, long pointed noses, and ears that twirled like small satellite dishes searching for a signal. A few more cars whistled by at speed, which made the pigs squeal even more, but they stood their ground. I got the impression they wanted to cross to the other side of the road, so I walked out to the middle of the road and stuck my arms out to stop the traffic, praying that the drivers would notice me. I'm pretty sure I must have looked like a crazy person but my plan worked. Drivers put on their hazard lights and cars stopped on both sides. After a couple of minutes, the pigs darted across the road to the safety of the forest on the other side. I so wish I could tell you they lifted a trotter in gratitude but, no, they bolted off into the undergrowth. I also wish I could tell you that the other car drivers applauded my actions, but mostly they just looked at me unsmilingly or rolled their eyes and drove off without looking back. No doubt they went home that day and told the tale of a mad woman who roams the forests ferrying pigs across the roads.

The countryside of Pas-de-Calais is a haven of nature, and I love that. Wild herbs grow at the side of the road, storks roost in the trees, and you can hardly tell their nests from the huge bundles of mistletoe that pepper the branches of trees in fields and forests. The local people really care about the countryside and when spring has almost sprung it often means towns and hamlets make time for a tidy-up. This March, when the mayor asked everyone to join a pre-spring 'clean the streets campaign', almost half the inhabitants of the village turned up on a chilly Sunday morning to get involved.

We were told to be there for 9.30 for a 10 a.m. start time. 'Half an hour warm-up?' I said to Mark. 'I wonder why.' Well, it turns out that it takes that long to kiss everyone hello and shake hands. We arrived with just fifteen minutes to spare, by which time the town hall *salle de fêtes* (party room) was full of people holding tiny plastic cups and knocking back strong black coffee, the sort that would keep you awake for a week. We walked the line of those already gathered, instinctively arranged in a sort of semi-circle, sharing pecks on the cheek. Right, left or right, left, right – to be truthful I have no idea what you're supposed to do, and some shake hands too, so you just have to watch carefully and respond in kind. Then we got on the end of the line and those who came after shuffled their way round, mwah-mwah-mwahing until they got to the end and we were all done. It took so long for everyone to get round that we didn't start the clean-up until well after ten o'clock.

Then the mayor made a speech, thanking us for turning up, told us to make sure we were wearing our hi-vis jackets (on account of the fact that a car might pass by), issued us each with a plastic sack and gave us instructions as to which roads to clean. We split into groups of four or six and off we went roaming the little *rues* and alleys to collect every shred of rubbish we could possibly find. Mark and I were in the non-French contingent, joined by a Dutch couple who live near the church. The sun shone, birds were singing in the hedge, and even Thierry's sheepdog, an old and remarkably shaggy collie with arthritic legs and a loud bark, came out to stare at the unusual level of activity on a Sunday morning.

I have to say, our clean-up outing didn't take long due to the fact that there are very few roads and they were already very clean. As we wandered, searching under hedgerows for something to throw in our bags, wild birds flew up in protest. We passed other groups of neighbours straying from their allotted routes, desperate to find some rubbish as if not doing so was a failure in citizenship. I am pretty sure that Jean-Claude went home and emptied a bin into his sack as he was the only person with a full load, which got him a cheer when we got back to the town hall.

The mayor then made another speech. I think there must be a French law about mayors making speeches if there are more than five people in a room. Afterwards, he offered us a choice of drinks – a glass of sparkling wine with a hint of cassis (blackcurrant liqueur) or a gut warming *genièvre*, a sort of gin that's made locally from juniper berries – definitely not for the faint-hearted. It made for a cheerful bunch at eleven o'clock in the morning.

This is a very jolly region, despite or perhaps because of the amount of rain that falls, and nothing illustrates this better than the Carnival of Dunkirk, right on the tip of northern France. It's not like other carnivals in France. In Nice and Menton, for instance, you'll find people throwing flowers, heralding the arrival of spring. In Annecy, people dress in Venetian costumes and wear masks, looking very sophisticated and gorgeous. In Dunkirk, they throw smoked herring and dress like pantomime dames. And, while the weather might not be as warm as the south when the winter months start to recede, you can definitely be sure of a warm welcome in the north. In its own way, the Carnival of Dunkirk is just as flamboyant and fabulous as the sunny southern festivities – just very different.

On a chilly Friday evening in Arnaud's bar, we sat at

a long table in the centre alongside some of the locals, including a couple we chatted to regularly called Chantal and Charles. We'll often stop at a bar on a Friday night, a tradition from our London lives where we referred to Friday as POET's day (Piss Off Early Tomorrow's Saturday) and a visit to the pub on the way home was normal.

'What do you have planned for this weekend?' asked Arnaud as he carried over a small beer for Mark and a *kir Pétillant* (sparkling wine with a blackcurrant liqueur) for me. The usual, we replied: working on the house, and preparing the garden for vegetables if it's not too wet.

'You do know it's carnival weekend, don't you?' said Arnaud's mum, who was sitting in the corner knitting and listening in on everyone's conversations, which she would then repeat to her friends later, embellished with her take on whatever was said. I don't ever say anything in the bar that I don't want the whole of northern France to know about.

'We've been before,' said Mark. 'It was cold, and mad.'

'*Bah oui,*' said Chantal, which is pretty much what every conversation starts with, though nobody knows what *bah* means. '*Bah oui,* it is crazy – but have you been as a Ch'ti?'

'*Bah non,*' I said, which got me a funny look.

Ch'ti is a term used to describe northerners who speak a sort of patois and have a strong accent. To be a Ch'ti is to be proud of your roots and your heritage – and to accept that no one knows what you're talking about. Often words are similar but different enough not to make a jot of sense, not just to non-natives but to the rest of France. For instance, *yeux* (eyes) is *yux*, *vache* (cow) is *vaque*. Some letters are dropped so *je* becomes *j'*, and the *s* sound become *sch*. So when someone speaks full-on Ch'ti you'll probably think either you are not in France any more or you have lost your mind. Or they have. A neighbour from Lille, just over an hour's drive away, who has a holiday home in our village, once told us he can't understand a word of Ch'ti and finds the locals impossible to comprehend. It was only when he saw a film called *Bienvenue Chez les Ch'tis* (France's biggest grossing film of all time and well worth seeking out) that he realized that all local speakers didn't have a speech impediment.

'You must come with us to the carnival on Sunday,' announced Chantal. 'We will make you Ch'ti it through our eyes. Mark can be Sam and drive us there in your English tank.'

Sam is the name given to a designated sober driver as it's the name of a character in a TV advertising campaign against drink driving in France. And the tank is the name our French friends have for our right-hand-drive 4 x 4. They are allegedly fascinated by the different driving position and like to experience it, though I suspect that they just want Mark to be Sam.

'Pick us up at ten in the morning,' were the instructions, and Chantal gave us her address.

We spent Saturday morning cleaning out our car, which serves as a cross between a builder's van and a tractor. It pulls the trailer with ease, the roof rack takes a load of weight and the roomy interior is always full of tools and DIY paraphernalia.

On Sunday morning we arrived at Chantal and Charles's farm on the outskirts of the little village of Zoteux, where we were met by the unlikely sight of Charles and two other men dressed like Aunt Sally dolls. They grinned at us, revealing teeth painted black. They tossed back the long blonde hair of their wigs and flounced across the muddy courtyard gingerly in their manly boots so as not to get splashes onto their torn stockings, meanwhile holding their miniskirts aloft and adjusting balloons under their tops. These were quite the weirdest pantomime dames I'd ever seen. I've no idea what the cows thought of them as they peered over the top of the railings of their barn.

Inside, Chantal tut-tutted at our lack of preparation. She herself was dressed in a teddy-bear suit. Bright feather boas were produced, Christmas hats were dug out and Chantal offered to do our makeup.

'Erm, no it's all right,' said Mark as we stared at Charles and his mates, who had come in from the cold.

The temperature had left their faces white so the bright pink freckles stood out, contrasting curiously with their Abba-ish blue eye shadow and lurid red lipstick. Charles introduced his farmer mates who would make their own way to Dunkirk – Denis and Louis, two strapping brothers with square jaws and muscles on muscles.

Dunkirk can seem industrial and grey. Of course, most of us know it for Operation Dynamo, the mass evacuation of allied soldiers in May 1940, or for its ferry port. But the centre is charming, the people are friendly and at carnival time there is absolutely nothing drab about it. Thousands upon thousands of locals turn out, as they have done for years, in the weirdest and brightest clothes that they can fit into. The carnival dates back to the seventeenth century when fishermen would leave for Iceland and the town held a send-off with a band, men dressed as women (to illustrate the point that there were no men left), and much beer drinking and singing. Nothing has changed. They love their heritage and patrimony here and hold on to traditions with fervour.

Despite thousands of people crowding the streets, we still managed to find free parking in the centre and joined the masses of revellers making their way to bars and restaurants before the carnival proper started after lunch.

Charles led the way to a small bar where we joined Denis and Louis. It was heaving with men dressed as pantomime dames and women dressed as animals, Bart Simpson, clowns and various other guises known locally as *cle'tche*, a Ch'ti word. They all brandished bright-coloured parasols on tall poles and were draped in feather boas, as were we, though we were the centre of attention because we were still wearing normal clothes.

Everyone had a glass of wine except for poor Mark, the designated driver. The noise was unbelievable – people were singing and talking at the top of their voices, and the anticipation in the air was palpable. When drinks were finished, we were herded to the next bar and then the next. By now everyone except Mark was very merry and Chantal declared we must eat to make sure we didn't peak too soon. She had already organized a table in a restaurant, though there was plenty of tempting street food. When we entered the brasserie the barman kissed us all on both cheeks and led us through a restaurant brimming with diners to a courtyard, which was also full. As he carried out a table and chairs the whole courtyard burst into song. Before they could finish, from inside the restaurant came another song, completely different and even louder.

'Which is best?' yelled the barman. 'Let the *Anglais* judge.'

Where could we start? We couldn't understand a word

– it was like being at the loudest football match in the world. We conferred. 'We have to be careful,' said Mark. 'We don't want to upset anyone.' So, I voted for the restaurant, Mark for the courtyard. It was a tie. It was a somewhat cowardly abstention, but this diplomatic approach got a loud shout of approval and we were given a cheer as our *moules* arrived in big steaming bowls accompanied by copious amounts of *frites*. Over lunch, Chantal, who came from Dunkirk but had moved to the Seven Valleys when she married Charles, explained that there are fifty-seven carnival songs and everyone knows them. Everyone, that is, except me and Mark. Some public buildings and even private homes open their doors and welcome carnival-goers in. These places are called *Chapelles*, which indicates 'friendly houses where you can get a drink'. But, however much you drink, you must always be respectful and well-behaved.

Watching Charles, Denis and Louis wiping their lips with their cuffs after lunch, and reapplying lipstick with a hand mirror passed from one to the other, is one of the most surreal sights I've ever seen.

Back outside, we could hardly move. The boisterous crowd had grown even bigger and noisier: it was now a colourful sea of nuns, sea captains, polar bears, spotty dogs and ladybirds, Amazonian tribespeople (despite the bitter temperature) and pantomime dames of all ages. Even some giants walked among them – there was one dressed as a Roman general who, with his wife, towered over the crowds (giants are a common sight at public events in these parts and the tradition dates back centuries). There was singing and the sound of a drumbeat could be heard, the noise rippling through the crowd as it made its way closer.

'Link arms quickly,' shouted Chantal, 'and don't let go!'

We did as we were told, as a smartly dressed, kilt-wearing drum major lurched into view, followed by a dancing crowd. Then suddenly everyone started to move forward with arms linked, forming a circle around the drummer, going in and out like the maddest hokey-cokey ever seen. People were yelling '*Enchanté*' ('Pleased to meet you') as we were pressed up closely together. The afternoon passed in a blur of dancing, singing, drinking in bars, laughing and kissing. I have never in my life been kissed as much as I was at this carnival. It certainly makes your cheeks rosy!

At five o'clock, just when I thought things couldn't possibly get any odder, Chantal led us dancing to the town hall, where the mayor stood above us on the balcony and revellers lined the windows of the majestic building. Whistles blew, horns beeped and the crowd chanted 'Give us the herring we deserve,' after which the mayor and the revellers at the windows threw hundreds of packets of smoked herring, an astonishing 450 kilos of them, to the waiting crowd below, who cheered loudly.

Sober Mark persuaded me to stay put in case I got lost in the crowds trying to catch the flying fish. The singing, drinking and dancing goes on all night, but our friends declared they were exhausted and, besides, they had to get up early the next morning to feed the cows.

'So, how did you like your carnival, Ch'ti style?' asked Chantal as we made our way back to the car.

'I can honestly say, I've never experienced anything quite like it,' I said, and I wasn't exaggerating. We might not have the early sun of the south, but the glow of goodwill blows the winter cobwebs far away, helped by an icy gale coming off the English Channel.

On the way home we slept, everyone snoring except thankfully for Mark at the wheel of the tank, happy that Charles had offered to drive the next year. We knew that this was going to be a tradition for us from now on. We were Ch'tis. And that is not something to be taken lightly as an outsider.

In a hamlet nearby live my friends Gary and Annette, a bonkers but lovely couple from the UK. There is a surprising number of British expats in the north. Like many who move to this part of France, they were first drawn here by the ease of travel offered by frequent ferries and trains to the UK, he said politely before resuming his shouting and being dragged back out of the room. Gary didn't know what to make of it, but at the same time this seemed so French, so *politesse*. *Politesse* doesn't just mean politeness, but etiquette and courtesy too, and it is important at every level of French society, even in the most bizarre situations. By decree of the mayor in the little town of Lhéraule in Picardy, you can be asked to leave the town hall if you don't conduct yourself with a minimum amount of politeness, such as saying '*bonjour*' and '*merci*'. The rules were adopted when a taxpayer was discourteous to a civil servant in 2011.

As a thank-you for helping her look after her chickens and other animals as her arm recovered, and to take my mind off losing Gregory Peck, one of my favourite roosters whom I'd had for years, Annette gave me a furry-footed chicken. We put it in a cage in the chicken pen to start with so it could get used to our other birds – they can be mean sometimes. Fat Cat was fascinated by the fluffy brown bird and stared intently through the wire. As far as I could tell he wanted to be friends. Unlike most cats he doesn't mind birds at all. He often lies on his back on a bench in the garden with blackbirds and robins landing next to him, and takes no notice of them whatsoever. I wonder sometimes if he has deep thoughts about the meaning of life and whether he is actually a cat at all, since he doesn't do very certainly wasn't up for sharing the ladies. But as the other cockerels are all escapologists who spend their time in the garden with their little harems, Roger Moore inherited the pen and most of the girls, no longer unplucky in love!

As March progressed the snow disappeared, followed by heavy rain, and finally blossom started to make an appearance on trees. The annual events calendar got under way, starting with the Rallye du Touquet, like a mini Le Mans but in the countryside. The racing starts from the smart town of Le Touquet-Paris-Plage and then zooms round the hills, hairpin bends and notoriously tricky roads of the Seven Valleys. The Paris-Plage add-on came from the fabulously named Hippolyte de Villemessant, the founder of *Le Figaro* newspaper, in the 1800s because the town was so popular with Parisians who loved its forests for hunting, shooting and fishing. The name stuck. The British upper classes soon discovered its charms and arrived in their droves, and Le Touquet (locals drop the Paris-Plage as it's a bit of a mouthful) became one of the most popular holiday destinations in the world for the rich and famous. Noël Coward, Winston Churchill, P. G. Wodehouse, Marlene Dietrich, Edith Piaf, Cecil Beaton and Ian Fleming all holidayed here. Fleming's iconic Bond novel *Casino Royale* was inspired by Le Touquet's casino. French bad boy and lover of Brigitte Bardot, Serge Gainsbourg, got his first singing break there at Flavio restaurant (it's still there) and Sean Connery signed his first James Bond contract in the town.

In the early 1930s, Le Touquet was home to the world's largest hotel, with 500 rooms and 50 apartments so large they had private swimming pools, butler's quarters, a kitchen and up to ten rooms for guests. Alas, the Second World War left most of it destroyed, its pools filled with mines. Nevertheless Le Touquet still has an air of elegance, with fabulous villas, art deco monuments, wonderful restaurants and a long esplanade where once Harry Selfridge, the obscenely rich owner of Selfridges in London, paraded the Dolly Sisters twins, both of whom he was allegedly 'seeing'. They were vaudeville dancers who had left America to perform at the Moulin Rouge in Paris, and were nicknamed 'The Million Dollar Dollies' for their allure over men. They in turn paraded their pet tortoises encrusted with 4-carat diamonds and precious stones, a gift from Mr Selfridge, whom they repaid by losing £4 million of his money at the casino.

The Rallye du Touquet heralds the start of the French Rally Championship season in France and is revered by French motor-racing fans as it attracts drivers from around the world. There is huge competition between villages, all vying to be included on the circuit. The race has been going for sixty years but our little village never got a look-in thanks to the unkempt roads and lack of pedestrianized walkways.

Three years ago, however, when a new mayor was elected, the main road through the village and all the side roads were given a makeover. The road was widened, new tarmac was laid, walkways and crossings were added. As a result, we have been included on the race route for the last two years.

Inclusion is never guaranteed, and the mayor warned locals to be prepared for the village not to be selected again. A sheet of green A4 paper was popped in our post box – essentially a metal box set in the wall of the woodshed, which was once a room where bread was made. (The old brick-built bread oven remains, though it's now a campsite for spiders.) Nothing is done by email here – the post box is chockful each week with the thrilling (to some) news of upcoming promotions and special offers at the supermarket. The post people in France have magic keys that can open all mailboxes. Occasionally the excitement reaches fever pitch when a brochure arrives announcing that the mobile tools-and-daily-basics wagon will be in the village, selling life's essentials from the back of a large lorry. I am not sure to whom they are essential as they include some decidedly odd items: fake, lurid-coloured nails for cats; bondage-style corsets; the worst children's dummies you ever saw – some with oversized Bug's Bunny-style gnashers that protrude from the poor kid's stuffed mouth, guaranteed to make old ladies gasp. There are questionable rubber posing pouches for men and even false teeth to fit all sizes. Great, said nobody ever.

The A4 notification informed us that the mayor hoped we would all play out part in presenting the village in the best possible light as the race administrators were visiting to make final checks. And would we please check to make sure there was no rubbish in the street as he and the inspectors passed, and that things looked tidy.

The day before the inspection, vigorous village gardener and jack-of-all-trades Jean-François did his rounds with more vigour than usual. He spends his days cutting the verges, trimming the hedges, clearing the leaves from the drains and wandering around the streets making sure everything is spick and span. Mayors have a budget for this sort of thing but, before the new mayor was appointed, it was never utilized. This mayor is not leaving any stone unturned in his attempt to drag us into the twenty-first century. He's even installed some lampposts in the village. Jean-François had been unemployed and unhappy for several years before the mayor gave him a break. He takes his job extremely seriously and everyone in the village really appreciates the change in him, as well as in the streets.

At the village crossroads, outside the town hall, which

was formerly the local school, Jean-François could be seen directing two ruddy-faced drivers in their tractors, equipped with huge cylindrical brushes. 'I want this whole village cleaned,' he was yelling above the loud engines. He followed first one of them, pointing out a clump of mud that had been missed, and then the other, gesticulating wildly. 'We'll have to go around again if you keep missing bits,' he was shouting to the crestfallen tractor drivers who were making faces of exasperation to each other when his back was turned. But they know by now that they will only be allowed to return to farming duties once Jean-François is satisfied with the state of the roads – and woe betide any farmer who drags mud in from a field after the clean-up. The road will have to be cleaned again.

The officials from the Rallye council arrived to be greeted by the mayor as they parked their cars in the new spaces in front of the town hall. Wearing his ceremonial sash, he guided them around the village. Despite the fact that they had already visited several times in previous years, formalities must be observed. The inspectors and the mayor, followed of course by Jean-François, wandered the course before returning to the town hall for a glass of wine.

Later, we saw Jean-François trudging up the hill to his home, sporting his usual mournful expression. 'How did it go?' Mark asked. Jean-François pushed back his cap, sighed deeply and said, 'Who knows? There was some dirt on the road by the chapel.'

Soon after the visit we received another A4 sheet of paper informing us that our village had been selected for the rally. And now the planning began in earnest. A meeting was held at the town hall, and the position of safety barriers and obstructions for the cars to navigate were discussed at length. A map of the village was pinned on the wall of the town hall office showing the proposed route and the spots where straw bales could go. Everyone had an opinion. Surely we should have hay bales outside Madame Bernadette's house? said one. No, they should go by the field where the water runs across the road when it rains, argued someone else, and another was adamant they must go in front of the school bus shelter. Jean-François tried sticking pins on the map to reflect suggestions until the map was so full you couldn't see the name of the roads.

Finally, after what felt like hours, the meeting was over, the placing of the hay bales and jobs for marshals on the day agreed. We walked home accompanied by Thierry, one of the farmers conscripted to clean the roads.

'Isn't that the same route as last year?' I said.

'*Oui*, it's the same route,' Thierry confirmed.

'So why did we have to go through such a long meeting to agree a route for this year?'

'Democracy,' he replied in the same tone, as if I'd asked why there are clouds in the sky.

The week before the weekend rally saw the closing of some footpaths and a noticeable increase in traffic as rally drivers, both professional and amateur as well as a few wannabes, sought to familiarize themselves with the route.

The day before race day was the official testing day and the roads were closed for several hours except to rally drivers. In between, there was a mad dash to the shops, as everyone knew there would be no deliveries to the village for three days. It was packed in the boulangerie and they were doing a roaring trade, with people buying several loaves to last the rally. I read somewhere that 320 baguettes are eaten every second in France – that's a stonking 10 billion a year. Eating bread is a national obsession and when people can't get it, such as when the baker goes on holiday, it is the cause of much moaning. The Tour de France once went through a town nearby and the thing that people remember most was that the boulangerie ran out of bread by three o'clock. With the rally coming, no one was taking any chances.

A marquee was erected at the back of the town hall, and the whole village echoed to the sound of industrious preparation. Straw bales were put in position, warning signs were hammered along hedges and verges, and red tape was strung outside gates as a warning not to come out.

Around a quarter of a million spectators arrive for the race – not in our village, of course, they would never all fit, but along the route and in the towns. Competition to lure crowds is intense and towns hold hog roasts and barbecues to tempt those who would be spending a long day watching speeding cars whizz by. One village held a *moules* and *frites* lunch, promoted like crazy on a Facebook page that most people in the area can't see as the internet is so slow and there is no mobile phone signal.

Jean-Claude, no fan of the mayor, though he can't remember why, decided to host a barbecue on the flat roof of his big garage overlooking the crossroads, opposite the town hall – a prime position to watch the race. His barbecues are legendary, so everyone accepted their invitation with astonishing alacrity. 'How on earth will you get everyone on the roof?' I asked Bernadette. 'Don't ask me,' she replied, casting a look of displeasure at her excitable husband. 'I think it's a crazy idea. We're all likely to fall through onto the van, the amount of people he's asked.'

'Can everyone get up the ladder to the garage roof?' I asked Jean-Claude nervously, conscious that the average age in the village is certainly in the high double figures. 'Madame Bernadette is coming *bien sur*, Monsieur and Madame Jupe from down the road, Petit Frère …' He stopped as it suddenly dawned on him that of course there was no way, all being over seventy, they would ever get up a ladder. Come to think of it, I don't think Jean-Claude would have an easy time of it either, though he is only sixty-two. 'We'll have the barbecue in the garden,' said Bernadette in a tone that did not invite discussion.

The next day the rally kicked off, heralded first by Jean-François, who walked the course, holding on to his hat as he went past us, checking that there was no debris on the road. Bent over against a gale, bits of twig hitting him on the head from trees thrashing about, bushy eyebrows threatening to blow away and eyes watering, he muttered, 'Bit windy out,' making everyone laugh.

Then a BMW with flashing lights came hurtling along with someone shouting incomprehensible gibberish through a loudspeaker in between loud wailing horns. It swept round the course and, shortly after, the souped-up novice drivers came speeding by. After a break, the serious drivers and professionals came roaring through, tyres squealing, to the delight of the cheering crowds who lined the road and hung out of windows to watch. My little office, which was once a pigsty, shook.

At noon silence fell: it was lunchtime. Even the rally stops for lunch. Jean-Claude fired up the barbecue, steaks and sausages sizzled, chicken charred and baguettes were buttered. The smell wafted across to the town hall and drew admiring glances from the crowds who were tucking into burgers and chips from a food truck. The afternoon passed peacefully and then the night-time rally began. The idea of being up on the roof to watch the cars race round in the dark had begun to appeal to some. Buoyed by wine and beer, Jean-Claude and Petit Frère (he's been called Little Brother all his life as he was the lastborn of ten children, even though he's now fifty-four) hauled out a ladder and leaned it against the wall. They grunted with the strain of climbing the steep wall, the rest of us holding our breath until they reached the top. They leaned over to take two chairs and enjoy the grandstand views, grinning at those of us left at ground level to watch the headlamps coming through the dark. But it wasn't long until we could hear the sound of snoring. The two of them had fallen asleep, wrapped up in blankets, oblivious to the sound of racing cars, faces lit gently by the light of one of the new lampposts. Mark climbed up to wake them, despite Bernadette's advice that 'They'll wake up when they're hungry.' They clambered down the ladder gingerly with stiff legs and got the loudest cheer of the day when they finally reached the ground. Not all challenges go at high speed!

Never quit your dream

APRIL IS AN unpredictable month in northern France. '*Avril fait la fleur, mai en a l'honneur,*' (April makes the flowers, May has the honours) say the French, an indication that it's time to get going on the garden. The French word for spring, *printemps*, comes from the old French *prins*, meaning first, and *temps* meaning weather. Buds appear on trees, hedgerows get a green fuzz and cherry blossom bursts into colour against a sky that isn't always covered in cloud. With almost an acre of garden, we always have plenty to do, not least thanks to the moles who dig holes, and the chickens who examine everything to see if it tastes good (except for weeds – they are discerning diners). Even the cats like to get involved, lying in the wheelbarrows watching me work or 'fertilizing' the bits I've just planted.

In this rainy region, and with a garden that was once two fields, one of which was inhabited by sheep, the growing conditions are perfect for two clueless gardeners who want to be self-sufficient.

Dad's birthday was 1 April. As dusk fell, we sat in the garden after a hard day of planting seeds, and, as we watched the pale spring sun dip behind the buttercup-covered hills of the Seven Valleys, we drank a toast to his and Mum's memory. Although they have been gone for a few years now, I think of them every day.

It's always out here that I feel the memory of Mum the strongest. She loved her garden and, when she died, we spread her ashes around her favourite tree – Dad could see it every day and feel that she was still there. I sometimes hear her voice in my head saying, 'Don't be like me – and never quit your dream.' When she found out she had terminal cancer just months after retiring, she was angry that she wouldn't have a chance to realize her dream to travel the world, or to be a writer, or to achieve so many of the others things that she'd planned for her retirement. I didn't even realize I had a dream before we bought the house, or even for a long time afterwards. It just simply felt like discovering the house was meant to be, and the fact that somehow I'd subconsciously always wanted something like this life for myself crept up on me.

Originally a cow barn with walls made of straw and mud, the house was extended over the centuries with concrete blocks. It's a real mishmash of rooms built on a hill. The *longère*, as a low farmhouse-style building is called, is 100 feet long. At one end, at the top of the hill, it's on a single level with low ceilings. The other end, down the hill, is on two levels with higher ceilings. Over the years it has developed from a one-room barn for animals (now our bedroom) and simply spread down the hill. No one before us seems to have thought about levelling the land. Ever. We essentially built a box within a box. Mark always said it would probably have been cheaper and quicker to knock it down and start again but we went with our hearts and have spent years renovating. After laying tons of concrete, replacing every window and thirteen doors, reinforcing an end wall that threatened to bring the house down, doing all the electrics and plumbing, fitting two bathrooms and a kitchen, building internal walls to create bedrooms, plastering, painting and shoring up sagging beams, it bears little resemblance to the neglected, filthy building we first saw.

It never occurred to me then that I wouldn't be working in an office until I was so old and worn out that I'd likely be too tired to do or be anything else. I still had twenty-five years ahead of me before I reached the official age of retirement. My dad was old-school working class, and his influence on me was strong. His mantra was you went to work and that was your purpose in life. You did whatever was necessary to put food on the table and pay the bills. He often worked two jobs at a time, jobs that he hated, but he did what he had to do. And he expected his kids to do that, too. Mum also worked hard: she was a home-help worker, looking after the elderly, but she taught herself maths and became an accountant at a library. Both were uneducated but intelligent and unfulfilled. Dad accepted it was his destiny. Mum was never happy about it. Throughout her whole life, she felt like she had missed out. She didn't give up on her dream, she just never had a chance to make it happen.

When the chance came along to do something different with my life, give up my day job and renovate the house – even if it was only planned to be for a short while before needing to return to normality and a job to pay the bills – I was scared and reluctant. It was Mark's daydream more than mine but he gave me the courage to take a risk – although on days when it was bitterly cold in our first winter and we had a deficient fire, I cursed him as we breathed out frost patterns inside the house! It was only when I started blogging that I realized that, buried deep, I did have a dream after all, a longing to write. My mum was a prolific writer, though she would hardly ever let anyone see anything she wrote. What I was allowed to read was wonderfully dark and full of magic (she was an Edgar Allan

Poe and Stephen King fan). When she discovered she was dying of cancer and didn't have long left, she deleted from her computer everything she ever wrote, saying she wasn't a good writer. It was heartbreaking.

I found that once I started writing, I didn't want to stop. I knew I had realized my *raison d'être*. It opened up a whole new life for me, and with it came the opportunity to discover more of France than I ever thought possible. A part of me feels like I'm fulfilling my mum's dream, too. And, in setting up a website for me to blog on, Mark also found his calling. He loved learning the technical skills needed, from understanding computer language to designing websites, search-engine optimization, what Google loves and a whole heap more.

We felt that we had plenty to celebrate as we sat there under a pink sky watching our chickens jump into trees, ready to roost for the night, and listening to pheasants squawking and cows mooing in the field at the bottom of the garden. We were all but finished renovating inside the house, and just had the outside to do. It had been a long, hard slog but we were so close to finishing.

April Fool's Day is known in France as *poisson d'avril* – April Fish Day – because it's customary for kids to stick a paper fish on your back. Their hope is that you'll walk around all day unaware of people tittering behind you!

Some historians say that April Fool's Day originated in France when the calendar was changed from the Roman Julian style to the Gregorian style in 1582, making the start of the new year 1 January instead of 1 April. Those who were slow to receive the news, who must have been plenty as it was mostly circulated by word of mouth, continued to celebrate the new year at the wrong time – the fools!

There are occasionally some fun prank stories in the papers but on the whole they're a bit lame. The best one I recall is reading that the French government was going to make it obligatory to carry a picnic basket in your car alongside the usual paraphernalia such as a high-viz jacket and spare bulbs. It was claimed the emergency picnic basket had to contain a bottle of wine, cheese and a baguette plus, of course, a red-and-white checked tablecloth. With all the madness that's going on in the world today, that's a law I could definitely get behind.

This time of the year is generally a little early for picnics in the north of France, unlike the south, but the village is always a hive of activity as villagers seemingly come out of hibernation to cut the grass, trim the rose bushes and tidy their gardens. I'm a morning person and like to get up in time to see the sun rise and listen to the birds sing. From the start of April, cuckoos were calling and every morning a blackbird sat in the sycamore tree outside my office in the former pigsty and whistled a whole raft of tunes. Sometimes he made a sound like a fire engine's siren, sometimes like a telephone ringing; he even trilled what sounded like the opening bars of Vivaldi's *Gloria*. Occasionally another blackbird joined in, copying the first one so that they sounded like a whistling tag team.

Not quite so beautiful a birdsong came from Fred and Florence, our rather rotund and very unfriendly Canada geese (named after Mark's grandparents who were lovely and not like the geese at all). They had been given to me by Jean-Claude along with Liz Taylor and Richard Burton, two Embden geese with bright blue eyes and mean tempers. That was before I realized that one day I wanted to live in Paris and that geese can live for more than twenty-five years. I am not sure that Parisians are ready for a neighbour with geese.

Every now and again stories crop up in French newspapers about city dwellers with holiday homes in the countryside taking their neighbours to court over noisy animals. Sometimes, it's the animal that's in the dock, as in the case recently of Maurice the cockerel, whose constant crowing drove the people next door crazy. He became something of a cause célèbre in France: thousands of people signed a petition to 'save Maurice' and T-shirts were made, sporting Maurice's photo and the words 'Let me sing'.

Thankfully the judge ruled in the cockerel's favour – he was allowed to stay and is happily crowing away each day. Other cases have seen donkeys, cows, ducks and even frogs with loud croaks come under fire. All I'll say is, if you think country life is going to be silent, you're in for a surprise.

At this time of the year our geese are very territorial and early in the month both girls and even one of the boys started nesting on a pile of twigs (which looks very uncomfortable) under a laurel tree. If we venture anywhere near them, even to put food in the pen, their panicked cries echo round the valley. On days when our Parisian neighbours were in residence, the cackling cacophony set off their dog, which set off our dogs, which then set off the entire neighbourhood of dogs. And since pretty much everyone has a dog here, the howling and barking made it sound like the village of the damned. Although we still had not seen the humans, the dog had escaped several times under the big wooden gate they had erected. Jean-Claude is convinced the Parisians did this 'so we can't see in'. He seems to believe that they were up to something worth seeing. Quite what that might be, he is not able to say. He's only been to Paris twice in his life and the last time was thirty years ago. 'I didn't like it then and I don't like it now,' he says. In vain I tell him Paris has changed, even from ten years ago. People are far friendlier, partly as a result of an effort by the tourist office to coach employees involved in the tourist industry to be more hospitable and to learn English. But mainly, I think, due to a number of tragic events that have brought Parisians together and made them thankful to the visitors who continue to come.

The dog, which to everyone's disappointment is not a poodle but a big-eared, pug-nosed *Bouledogue français*, likes to run down the alley from its house, into the road which run through the village, and confront the admittedly rare cars and tractors that pass by. 'Typical Parisian,' said Jean-Claude.

The geese found plenty to shout about when one morning I discovered that Mariah Carey, the Barbary duck with a high-pitched squeak, had hatched some eggs. This is something the geese have never managed to do, and neither had the chickens at that point. Since the end of March, after a relatively mild winter, some of the birds had started nesting in earnest as the weather improved. There were broody chickens hogging the coops, and ducks sitting on eggs under hedges, in the big flowerpots and in the field at the bottom of the garden. Sometimes I saw them sneaking back in for food and water or scuttling onto the terrace to pinch the cats' food. They weren't alone in this pilferage – a hedgehog family visited every night, scoffing and snorting and pushing the cats out of the way. They have been coming for a few years and bring their offspring every year.

The little birds had clearly only just hatched and were very lucky to have survived. One was pale yellow; the other, a boy, was black with yellow markings. We took them home and put them in a cage with a heat lamp to keep them warm. They were friendly and tame as anything. We called them Barbie and Ken and for the next four weeks they stayed in the house with us, being pampered and spoiled, until they were big enough to go into a nursery pen in the garden and get used to the fact that they weren't alone.

It was Easter by now, so they weren't the only eggs that crossed our path. It's pretty much the law to eat chocolate at this time of the year in France. Chocolatiers all over France display fabulous chocolate concoctions in windows and the delectable scent inside the shops is enough to break the will of the most fastidious dieter. Legend has it that on the Thursday before Easter Sunday, French church bells fly to Rome to see the Pope, and no bells ring during that time. On the way back to France, aiming to arrive in time to ring for Easter Sunday, the bells collect chocolate goodies and drop them for children en route. And so it's the chocolate bell, rather than the chocolate bunny, that's the star here. We headed to the town of Montreuil-sur-Mer where the artisan chocolate shop in the square was packed with little old ladies buying their Easter treats, and children who were allowed to choose just one thing: it's about quality not quantity here. Each year, there are handmade chocolates, intricate chocolate sculptures and huge blocks, some with nuts or fruit, which you buy by weight with the server taking up a small hammer to chip off a piece. The lady who works in the shop always gives customers the choice of one of her handmade chocolates when they have made a purchase. It's a tradition I really like!

With the more frequent blue skies of spring, we turned our attention to outside jobs and working off some of the calories from the chocolate. The house had to be rendered, a job we'd been dreading. Many of the older houses in the village use lime render, a building material that dates back as far as Roman times. But in the nineteenth century, more modern materials such as cement and mortar mixes became popular. Luckily for us, the fact that our house is enclosed by cement blocks meant we didn't need to use lime render, a slow process to make and apply. With our long house, it would have taken many months to do.

For years we'd discussed having smooth cream-coloured walls. Half of the house at the front had dull grey blocks and half was already rendered in a grey stipple, which we intended to smooth out. Confronted with the reality of the long wall of the house, however, we decided just to cover the blocks and paint the stippled render. Even that was a big job. I mixed the render in a big bucket, and

Mark applied it to the wall. We started as the sun came up and finished when the sun went down. You can't have joints when you're rendering, and it dries quickly so it's a race against time, and we only had around half an hour per bucket. There were three coats to apply and we started with the biggest wall, which is 30 feet long, knowing that we would run out of energy.

On the first day, Monsieur Martel went by on his way to see Madame Bernadette and stopped to watch for a while.

'Doing a nice job there,' he said admiringly. 'My place could do with a new coat, you know.'

'No chance,' said Mark without stopping to raise his head from the sweeping of plaster to wall.

'I had a man come and do my walls once, it took him three months,' said Monsieur Martel. 'It was in 1967,' he explained.

'I don't care if it was 1867,' said Mark. 'When I'm done with this lot, I'm done.' I couldn't blame Mark. It was back-breaking lifting heavy buckets of render, moving the scaffolding along, reaching up high to the top of the walls and bending down to the bottom.

Monsieur Martel laughed and carried on his way with an easy smile. It had been worth a shot.

Shortly after, Monsieur Henri, Thierry the farmer's father, came wandering along, dressed in his pyjamas and slippers as usual. He has Alzheimer's and the family care for him at home, with the help of a nurse from time to time, but every now and again he escapes and goes for a walk. Not very far, thankfully, and everyone knows him so he just gets taken home when he's spotted.

As he came into the garden, he stopped to watch Mark working. After a few minutes he went and got one of the garden chairs, placed it next to Mark and sat down to make himself comfy. 'Hold on there for five minutes,' said Mark, 'and I'll take you home.'

Monsieur Henri just smiled. Sometimes he says nothing, sometimes he talks but he has a very strong accent and often mixes up his words. We don't understand him and he clearly doesn't understand us either, but he seemed pretty happy sitting there quietly.

As soon as Mark finished, he took the old man's arm and we led him to the gate to take him home up the hill. Thierry's mad sheepdog barked as we approached and the nurse came running out of the house. '*Mon Dieu*,' she said, 'again with the walking off!' and took his hand to take him back home.

At the end of three days during which Monsieur Martel and several neighbours stopped to watch, we had the first wall done and knew we'd made the right choice simply to paint what we could.

We had permission to paint the house and to instal shutters. There aren't any rules about colours in our village as there are in some places. On the Île de Ré, for instance, you can only choose from a palette of sixteen shades – eight blue and eight green. But we did have to notify the mayor and the town-planning authorities that we intended to change the appearance of the outside of the house. Thankfully not all the windows needed shutters but there were still thirty-two to paint, four coats of Wedgewood Blue on each side, adding a little Provençal-style colour here in the north. As Mark rendered, my job was painting and I knew it would take me the whole of the rest of spring and summer to complete if I started now.

Jean-Claude, who keeps a very tidy house and garden with plenty of instruction from his wife, walked by while I was painting and gave me an approving nod. Our house had been an eyesore for decades but, bit by bit, it was changing.

Spring is when the flea markets, called *brocantes*, *marchés aux puces*, *vide-greniers* (literally 'empty your attic'), *réderies* and *braderies*, begin in earnest. They are a way of life in France. In my department alone, there are more than three thousand flea markets a year. Most take place from March to early autumn. Some are small affairs, just a couple of meagre stalls with a few locals selling their unwanted kitchen utensils, clothes and kids' toys outside their homes.

Others are huge, like the Lille Braderie, with around ten thousand stalls. This thirty-six-hour, non-stop event has a party atmosphere and bargain hunters come armed with torches to carry on through the night. It spreads for miles, through cobbled streets, down wide avenues and onto squares large and small. At the same time, restaurants hold a competition to see who can sell the most *moules* dishes, proudly piling empty mussel shells outside as proof, sometimes a mountain of them. About 2 million visitors descend on the city, and if you like flea markets, you'll be in seventh heaven at this one.

Flea-market aficionados largely fit into three different camps. The first are serious shoppers, antiques dealers and online shop owners looking for treasures to upsell. They attend the specialist markets dedicated to postcards, stamps, militaria and antiques as well as local flea markets, hoping to find a Renoir or a Monet, hidden away in an attic for centuries. It happens. Not long ago, a family who lived near Toulouse found a long-lost painting believed to be by Italian painter Caravaggio; it was valued at the time at 120 million euros. You can bet your life when that story appeared in *Le Figaro* newspaper, people all over France were checking their attics for treasures. Just a few years before that, a ninety-year-old woman, who was selling her house in Compiègne in Picardy, called in a local auction company to dispose of belongings. The young auctioneer who arrived, just a year into the job, spotted an intriguing painted wooden panel above the hot plate of the old lady's oven. He decided to research it and it turned out to be an old masterpiece dating back over seven hundred years. Depicting a scene from Christ's Passion, it was by a thirteenth-century Florentine painter known as Cimabue, and valued at over 5 million euros.

Then there are those who are obsessed with collecting things. They visit several *brocantes* each weekend, travelling from town to town seeking a bargain. They include sharp-elbowed little old ladies who will nudge you out of the way if they spot something special – they're certainly not going to let you get in their way. Gary and Annette also fall into this category.

They live in an old building, a former village schoolhouse of several rooms, a cellar and multiple outbuildings. Every room in the house is filled to overflowing with all sorts of things. Medals, uniforms, books and ancient newspapers are Gary's penchant. He's a retired electrician turned historian and battlefield guide, and sports an extended, imperial-style bushy moustache with curled ends and mutton-chop sideburns. He looks like an ageing Freddy Mercury. Annette, a rosy-cheeked former matron, cannot resist the lure of antique clothes, buttons, magazines, knitting patterns, glass, china, perfume bottles, kitchenalia, ornaments and much (much) more. Every Sunday they set off in their car with a goal to visit two *brocantes* before lunch and two more after lunch. They are bargain hunters extraordinaire and their car is normally fit to burst with their buys. When I visit their house, I wonder how much more they can possibly buy as every inch of their home is full. They converted an old stable block into a dining room and study but that's now full, so they're considering converting a huge barn, currently the playroom of two goats and umpteen chickens.

And there are others, who like us, are happy just to wander and browse. Mark likes to look at militaria; I like to look at almost everything else. We're constantly amazed by the often hideous, the frequently weird, and the frankly downright odd. You will, more often than you would ever think possible, see leaking, long-dead stuffed animals, the ugliest dolls in the world – they would give Chucky a run for his money – or used wine-bottle corks. On the other hand, I have bought some real gems, including an antique typewriter for a few euros, though Mark didn't think of it quite as fondly as he had to carry it a mile back to the car. I also bought a huge threadbare but beautiful tapestry in a frame that was too big to fit in the car, so we had to tie it on the roof where it flapped all the way, making everyone we passed turn in amazement. I've even come home with a cat and a cockerel.

Mark is a fairly reluctant flea-market-goer. There's always the issue of parking to start with. A good *brocante* can lure hundreds to a small high street. Diversions are usually in place to deal with the traffic, and a uniformed official (think hi-vis jacket and whistle) will be directing a long line of cars full of impatient treasure hunters. On the whole, French people have an aversion to walking, except in Paris where walking is de rigueur, so parking more than hundred metres from a *brocante* brings out the worst in drivers. They will park in the middle of a roundabout, around a roundabout, at odd angles sticking out in the road at junctions, across gates clearly marked no parking and even on pedestrian crossings.

A *brocante* is also a day out for the stallholders. People set out tables and blankets in the road in front of their homes. Several generations of the family will be present, sitting at picnic tables, enjoying an all-day barbecue, chatting with neighbours and friends, bartering over 50 centimes for that pre-loved item.

For keen gardeners, flea markets are a good place to get young plants, especially tomatoes and salads, as well as flowers grown by green-fingered locals. Our plans to grow our own vegetables as much as possible weren't exactly successful due to lack of time but we were determined this was going to be the year, buoyed by the trays of plants we could buy at the *brocantes*. The greenhouse that I'd bought on eBay years before and dismantled, before transporting it to France wrapped in copious amounts of newspaper, was filled with seedlings and plants including some wild garlic we'd found growing prolifically in the Forest of Desvres on the outskirts of Boulogne-sur-Mer. At certain times in spring, you'll find the forest full of foragers, keen to pick some of the strong-scented flowers and leaves for soups and salads. Jean-Claude makes a garlic soup that's so strong you could probably light a fire with your breath after just a small bowl. The locals say that the garlic was planted by the Romans. Julius Caesar set sail from the beaches of Boulogne in 55 BC to conquer Britain and I love to think of the Roman emperor telling his commander to get some garlic ready for when he came back, and that I'm now picking from its offspring two thousand years later.

Although we can walk for miles browsing the *brocantes*, I knew I had to up my exercise because, like Madame Bernadette, I seem unable to resist cakes – and also wine, cheese, bread, chocolate and a few more things. The good life was definitely starting to take its toll on my waistline. And in this land of rolling hills and forests, it's no hardship to walk the dogs for an hour twice a day. It meant I saw more of the wildlife – deer, wild pigs, hedgehogs, moles, Lady Amherst's pheasants (no, she's not a local but that's what the colourful birds are called), rabbits and hares – since it frequently crossed our path as we traipsed through the woods and valleys. One morning three small grey owls accompanied us, flying from tree to tree along the path. The dogs thankfully have little or no chance of catching anything as they streak across the fields and up and down the hills – the wildlife here is tough and used to making a quick escape. On a rather damp April morning, however, they did make a catch – of sorts.

As the mist hung like wet cobwebs over the valley, we set off for our walk, out through the main street of the village (don't get excited, it's only eighteen houses), and up a small hill past the tiny private chapel where the road branches off. One way leads to the fields where Thierry the farmer grows sweetcorn and potatoes, peas and cabbages. The other way leads to a small alley with a couple of tiny cottages. We always go the way of the fields. The dogs know this and they never deviate. With that day being the exception. All three of them ran down the alley barking excitedly.

Both of us yelling at them didn't make any difference at all. This is not uncommon when I shout – no one takes any notice of the maid – but they are usually better behaved for Mark. Clearly both being ignored this time, we took off in hot pursuit of the dogs, following the sound of wild woofing. To our surprise we were confronted by a very large white cow with black spots in the small, flower-filled front garden of one of the cottages. The dogs were utterly thrilled at their discovery. They were running around in circles, wagging their tails and panting with joy. The cow wasn't remotely bothered by the attention. She lifted her big head slowly, stared for a second with soft brown eyes and, dismissing us all, ducked her head to carry on eating the pretty flowers.

The dogs barked as we stood there wondering whether we should knock on the door or if that might make the cow rampage and do more damage. We didn't have to wait long. A pepperpot-sized old lady with a bun of white hair and little round glasses opened the front door of the house and stuck her head out.

'*Merde*,' she said loudly when she saw the huge beast munching away. She disappeared back into the house. A short while later, she came out carrying a length of rope, rolled her eyes at us and, not remotely bothered by the size of the cow towering above her, tied the rope around her neck and then attempted to pull her off the flowers. That was never going to happen. The cow wasn't moving. Not one inch. She didn't even lift her head to look.

'*Bonjour Madame*,' I called, 'can we help?'

The old lady beckoned us into the garden. 'If you push with me,' she said, looking at me, 'and you pull,' she instructed, looking at Mark, 'perhaps we can move her.'

So there I was at the back end of a cow, trying to avoid being pooed and peed on next to a tiny old lady, while the dogs, silent now, watched on.

After a few seconds of making absolutely no progress, she said, 'Wait there. I will get my old man,' and disappeared back into the house, leaving Mark and me standing in the garden. She shortly returned and introduced her husband. He was tiny, too.

Mark was now relegated to the cow's backside alongside me, while Monsieur and Madame Pepperpot pulled on that rope for all they were worth. At this, the cow got the hump and started mooing, grass and flowers falling from its enormous gnashers. The dogs seemed to enjoy this immensely. Ella Fitzgerald started howling and then Churchill and Bruno joined in.

That did it. The cow looked up from her floral feast and blinked. We instinctively seized our chance and heaved as hard as we could. The Pepperpots tugged with all their might. The beast lurched forward with a surprised look in her eyes.

'Don't stop,' yelled the tiny old lady. 'Keep pushing … get her round the side of the house and into the field.'

We finally got that bugger back into the pastures from which she had escaped. Evidently a gate had been left open (Madame Pepperpot narrowed her eyes at her husband). We were invited in for coffee, so Mark put the dogs in the front garden and made sure all the gates were shut before stooping to enter through the small front door. At over six feet tall he could hardly stand in the tiny kitchen, with its low ceiling festooned with pots and pans of all shapes and sizes. The smell of coffee from a pot heating on the wood oven filled the room. The flower-patterned wallpapered walls were chock-a-block with cupboards and dressers, and a small table and four rickety old chairs sat in the centre of the room. An ancient spaniel woke up from its slumber in front of a roaring wood fire, wagged its tail and wandered over to sniff us. A solitary canary sat in a cage by a small window overlooking the errant cow's field. The cow was leaning her head over a fence, with a donkey and a goat on the other side. It looked as if she was telling them about her adventure.

Monsieur Pepperpot, whose name we discovered was Jean, poured the coffee – strong and thick, guaranteed to keep us awake that night. The old couple chatted away in a heavy local accent, but seemed to be talking slowly so that we could understand. Madame Pepperpot, who was really Agathe, told us they were in their seventies, had been childhood sweethearts and married for more than sixty years. As they chatted Jean constantly patted her arm and Agathe rubbed her hand through his mop of white hair.

'We used to be cow farmers like our parents before us and their parents before them. But we're too old really and we've only got the three cows now,' said Jean, adding that their only son, like so many in French rural communities, had left decades before to work in an office in a city and now lived in Toulouse. Every winter they spent time with him there and kept their cows in the barn of a friendly farmer nearby.

'We've got a trailer,' said Jean, sighing, 'but getting those beasts onto it isn't easy sometimes …'

'Well,' said Mark, 'we'd be happy to help you. We seemed to have managed pretty well between us.'

'*Bien sûr*,' I said, 'of course.'

Madame Pepperpot gave us a litre of fresh cow's milk when we left.

If you had told me just a few years ago that, one day, I'd be shoving the rear end of a cow, accompanied by an orchestra of barking dogs and led by a tiny old lady in a garden in middle-of-nowhere France, I'm not sure I would have believed you.

The house where the pigs live

MAY DAY FELL on a Monday, which pleased everyone since last year it had fallen on a Sunday, which had pleased no one as it meant no extra day off. In France, the date the national holiday falls on is the day you get off, even if it happens to be on a weekend.

As well as being International Workers Day, it's also the *Fête du muguet* in France. On the first of May in 1561, France's King Charles IX was given a *muguet* flower, a lily of the valley in English, as a lucky charm. He loved the idea so much he was inspired to offer the delicate white bloom each year to the ladies of the court. The practice spread and these days the flowers are sold in bouquets or as potted plants all over France in May. It's common for people to give lily of the valley to friends or family members for good luck.

I've been told that in some parts of France it's also traditional for young men to place a tree outside the door of someone they love during the night before 1 May. We're not talking a pot plant here. Imagine waking up to find you can't get out of the house because your admirer has put a tree in front of the door!

For the first time since the beginning of the year, we had lunch outside. When we had renovated the old pigsty, which had been no more than three walls and a falling-down roof, we had effectively created a small courtyard between it and the front of the house by turning it into an enclosed building. With shutters laid out on work benches covering most of the courtyard, there was just room for a table and two chairs. Several small worker bees came out of their hive from somewhere in the garden to look at the humans. There are naturally formed beehives everywhere in the village, mainly in concrete blocks in walls or in outbuildings. We just leave them be (no pun intended) and they leave us be, too.

The cats hovered around our legs, purring and rubbing their ears against us to get attention and scraps, noses in the air sniffing hard. The dogs barked from their bit of the garden at the back of the house as the aroma of our breakfast carried on the gentle breeze. Nearby, a cuckoo sang non-stop and the talented, whistling blackbird in the tree in the front garden made noises like a telephone. We planned our day ahead: more rendering for Mark, more painting of shutters for me and then I had some writing to do. May Day or not, we were determined to get on with the renovating. We also dropped off a lily of the valley plant for Bernadette, who ushered us through the house and into the garden where Jean-Claude was sitting, drinking a tiny cup of coffee.

I did initially wonder whether I was alone in my fondness for chickens as pets since, in this village, there is much boasting about the delights of someone's coq au vin or their duck à l'orange – everyone seems to keep birds for the pot. So, it was a huge surprise to discover that Jean-Claude – despite thinking I was crazy for crying when my first cockerel died – keeps some chickens purely for fun.

'I'm thinking that this one is pretty enough to win a contest,' he said, pointing at a large chicken that was waddling about in an ungainly manner. '*Un Soosecks*.' (A Sussex white to you and me.) 'Look at those glossy feathers, those strong fine legs, the clear eyes and red neck, just like my lovely wife,' crooned Jean-Claude. 'I think I will show her at the big town fair.' I think he was referring to the chicken, not the wife.

The big town, Hucqueliers, is about 5 miles away. It's where we all meet for major local events such as flea markets and the annual fair. Lots of farmers take their best-looking animals to show and sell, and crowds of visitors guess their weight, age and even name – we make our own entertainment here.

Bird showing is immensely popular at the fair, with cages laid out in a row, full of beautiful and often unusual-looking chickens. Some have what look like furry boots or bouffant hairstyles, others quirky or colourful plumage. Their proud owners sit alongside, watching the visitors ooh and ah, and nodding with satisfaction when buyers approach to place orders. These birds are keepers and can be quite expensive.

'Better yet,' continued Jean-Claude, 'I think my Soosecks could even win the beauty contest.' He went to pick Soosecks up, and she pecked meanly at him and squawked loudly.

Jane-Claude likes to pull my leg from time to time, but Bernadette assured me he was deadly serious and that in France there is a famous competition called 'Miss Poule et Mr Coq' (usually with the English forms of address). Apparently it's like a Miss World and Mr Universe combined – but for chickens. 'No chance,' said Bernadette 'The winner is always the one that has a sunny nature, and that bird is bad-tempered and proper bossy.' With that she strode off to the kitchen to make us all coffee.

'See, just like my lovely wife,' said Jean-Claude, but quietly, in case she heard him.

Later in the day, I was sitting in the pigsty, daydreaming about which of my chickens might be good enough to enter the Miss Poule contest and writing about beautiful Burgundy, which I had recently visited. It was peaceful at home, as usual. You could count the number of cars that go by our house each day on two hands if you don't include the tractors from the farm at the top of the road. Suddenly there was a really loud noise. It sounded a bit like the quad bikes of the locals as they ride round the country lanes, but I couldn't place it. I went to the front door – the sound was louder, but strangely it didn't seem to be receding like it would if it was a quad bike driving away.

I stepped out into the courtyard and there, above my head, was a huge swarm of bees. I have never seen anything like it before or since. There were thousands and thousands and thousands of bees buzzing about. Terrified, I ran into the house and called out for Mark, who was making a cup of tea in the kitchen. He must have heard the panic in my voice, as he came into the hall instead of yelling 'What?' from the kitchen like he normally does.

'Get the dogs in, quick,' I shouted. 'Close the windows. Close the doors. Get the cats in. Oh my god, the chickens!'

I was running around like a headless chicken myself trying to see how many cats were in the house.

'What on earth are you doing?' asked Mark, looking at me with a worried expression.

'Bees … bees …' I said. 'There are thousands of them swarming over the top of the pigsty.'

It was a biblical sight, and by now the swarm had cast a shadow over the courtyard. To my horror, I could see that I'd left the door of the pigsty open. And those bees were clearly looking for somewhere to live. Mark, being far braver than me, dashed across the courtyard and slammed the door shut before running back to the house.

We looked online for what you should do when bees swarm above your head. Apparently, the answer is: nothing. They won't hurt you and are most likely looking for somewhere to start a new hive. They're probably stuffed with honey, which makes them docile, and they're generally not aggressive. There were a lot of maybes. I didn't feel particularly reassured.

After about ten minutes of dramatic bee swarming around and over the top of the house, into the back garden and over the hedge into our neighbour Paul's garden, they simply left.

An hour later, I was writing that, in Burgundy, good food is on everyone's lips. Not literally, of course, but if you go to Burgundy and chat to the locals, it won't be long until the conversation turns to food – from the best wine for poaching eggs, to how to make proper boeuf bourguignon (opinion is divided over whether it's best to cook a whole piece of beef or do it in cubes à la Julia Child, the great American cook). Burgundians can talk endlessly about where the best markets are and where to buy the most scrumptious gingerbread. I was so engrossed thinking back to the market in Dijon – one of the best to which I've ever been – that when the droning noise returned outside, I didn't realize for a few moments that the bees were back. The light was still pouring through the windows, so although the noise was by now very loud, they were clearly not above the pigsty yet. Deeming it safe to leave the building, I opened the gate and looked into the road that runs along the front of our house. There was the swarm, swirling over Monsieur and Madame Jupe's house and garden opposite. I could hear the couple in the garden chatting away animatedly and the clink of wine glasses. It was May Day after all. Blimey, I thought, they're so laid-back about having 20,000 bees above their heads … How very French.

I watched as the mass of bees twisted and spun, whirling about Monsieur Jupe's car, parked at the side of the house, and over the top of the small chicken pen in the garden, which also contained Madame Jupe's horrible goose that attacks people whenever it escaped.

All of a sudden I heard someone shouting: '*SACRÉ BLEU! MON DIEU! REGARDEZ!*' followed by shrieks and the sound of a door being slammed loudly. Apart from the buzzing of the bees, there was now complete silence. Clearly my neighbours were not that laid-back.

Eventually the bees buzzed off. Jean-Claude told me that they had settled in the garden of a house nearby, and a local beekeeper had put up a box to catch as many as he could to give them a new home. Never a dull moment round here – always a hive of activity.

It was most likely, said Jean-Claude, the lovely weather we were having that brought the creatures our way. It wasn't until much later that I realized that not all of them had flown away. That summer a busy little bunch of them were evident in the courtyard, going in and out of the roof of the pigsty. We asked Jean-Claude what to do about them. 'Nothing really,' was his advice, giving a Gallic shrug. 'They are in the walls now, so unless you want to take the walls down they will stay there until they are ready to leave. They won't hurt you if you don't hurt them.'

So now we share the pigsty and the courtyard with the bees. Unlike wasps, they don't try to join us for a drink or food. In fact, they don't come anywhere near us. The only time they seem to be bothered is when I put a light on to

pick my way across the courtyard before the sun is up —
then they come out to have a look.

Monique, who sometimes helps Arnaud out in the bar
when Madame Armandine is away, hasn't been so lucky.
She had a hornets' nest in her garage. These big flying bugs
are aggressive stingers. Monique called the mayor, as we
are all encouraged to do when hornets' nests are involved.
They have become more prevalent in France in recent
years, and the Asian hornets in particular are feared here.
In some towns, such as ours, the mayor takes responsibility
for getting a professional in to deal with the intruders. 'But,'
complained Monique, 'it took two days and I had to keep
my little darling in the house all that time as I was afraid
she would be stung, and I couldn't bear to lose her.'

Monique's *petit chou*, which means little darling, a
misnomer if ever there was one, is a snarling, yappy and
precocious Chihuahua. Everyone hates the nasty little
creature when Monique brings it to work with her in the
bar. Even Madame Armandine's huge dog Beau doesn't
like it, and he loves everyone. Petit Chou has a variety
of jewelled collars, which are chosen to match whatever
colour dress or top Monique is wearing. When it comes to
work with her, she ties it to a chair in a corner and we all
steer clear of it. It used to be behind the bar with Monique,
but Arnaud trod on it once by accident, so now it has to

be in Monique's eyeline and away from big feet. You can't tell Monique that it's the nastiest little dog you've ever met as she is as fierce as it is, and unless you want your drink served with a scowl and no olives, you'd better be sure to say Petit Chou is a delightful creature. Just don't put your fingers anywhere near its teeth.

Monsieur Dubarre, a long-time regular, has been trying to teach Beau to bark every time he hears the word 'president' and has claimed some success with Petit Chou, though to tell the truth, she barks when the door of the bar opens, and when someone talks, laughs or moves. When Nicolas Sarkozy was in power, the chat in the bar was all about his style, his hauteur, his love of bling and his glamorous wife. If you had heard the inside knowledge that everyone appeared to have, you would have been fairly certain that many from the village moonlighted as spies and may even have been part of Sarkozy's inner circle of advisers, spending all week listening in on top-secret conversations. When François Hollande was president (or Monsieur Flanby, as some prefer to call him in a nod to a blancmange dessert that's sold in supermarkets here) it was the same. Despite protesting that everyone is entitled to privacy, the French love juicy gossip as much as anyone.

When President Macron was voted in, in 2017, there was much excitement as he's a 'local'. Well, sort of. He was born in Amiens in Picardy and has a home in Le Touquet–Paris-Plage.

Most people seem to think that it's a good thing that the first couple have kept their home here, because our little department is getting attention that it doesn't normally receive and hopefully people will see that it's more than just the rainy back of beyond that everyone seems to think it is. Others think he's forgotten his roots, but Monsieur Dubarre is a fan. 'Before you judge,' he says wisely, 'you should walk a mile in someone else's shoes.' He then spoils it somewhat by adding, 'Once you've done that, you can say what you like – they're a mile away and you've got their shoes.'

He says Macron outranks Sarkozy simply by dint of the fact that he likes cheese – the latter was not a fan of *fromage* at all. Your typical Frenchie will eat almost 26 kg of cheese – every year. Almost half the French eat it daily. Apparently there are around a thousand different types of cheese produced in France now – cow, goat, sheep and even horse's milk cheese, though the latter is not wildly popular.

Bars in our area seem to be closing with alarming regularity, the long-suffering owners tired of the ever-increasing and onerous paperwork. We used to go to one that was basically in the front room of a house that was open to the public.

There were once hundreds of these types of at-home bars in the region, but now there is only a handful. We see it as our duty to support the bar owners and community lifelines, and try to visit one of our favourites each week – at least, that's our excuse. There's not much that beats sitting in a cosy bar with friendly locals or sitting outside on a terrace watching the world go by in the sun with a glass of something chilled, saying *bonjour* and *au revoir* as people come and go.

Jean-Claude had said that the weather was going to remain good, so we were pretty sure we were in for a bad spell. We were right. Everyone always thinks that the Brits are obsessed with the weather, but the French are just as bad, if not worse. The day after Jean-Claude predicted that fine weather was here to stay, we passed him while walking our soggy dogs, our hair and clothes dripping, while he stood under his porch, surveying the rain gushing down the hill outside his house. 'Bit wet today,' he commented as we passed.

The next morning there he was again, wiping his feet on an old towel as he was about to go into his little cottage. (Bernadette is very house-proud and woe betide anyone who makes a mark on her floors.) 'Bit wet today,' he said, 'and humid.' We had 91 per cent humidity that day. It was more like being in the jungle than in a northern French hamlet.

never been to a supermarket in her life, grows all her own vegetables, keeps chickens and ducks, and goes for a walk every day without fail. She keeps her house absolutely spotless, and I often see her polishing the already gleaming windows or scrubbing the doorstep. She's never been on a plane or train; the furthest she's been outside the village is to the local hospital 20 miles away. But she is as obsessed with the weather as the rest of my neighbours and sits watching the daily hour-long *Météo à la carte* programme on TV. So, as I was off to Carcassonne the next day to research the best things to see and do (I love my job), I decided to pop in and ask what the weather would be like.

Claudette lives in the next house up the hill to mine. She was born in the house in 1933 and, when she got married, her husband moved in. It's where she gave birth to her only daughter, Bernadette, and nursed her seventy-year-old brother until he sadly passed away a couple of years ago. It's the biggest house in the village, and when the German army occupied this area, officers were billeted there. She's told me in the past that they were very polite and very nice to her and gave her sweets, which her mother told her off for taking. When I sit with her in the kitchen, she tells me stories of her life, of the village and the people that lived here. 'In that room behind you were two young German officers. They liked to smoke, which used to make my mother angry. We once had a party in this room and we played music on the record player [which is still there] and danced to *yé-yé* music for hours.' *Yé-yé* is what French people call music of the 1960s, apparently because of the phrase 'yeah yeah', heard in British music at the time.

She also often talks about the food she prepared there and how her mother taught her to cook. She never weighs ingredients and doesn't possess modern equipment such as a blender or mixer. Everything she prepares is measured by eye, guessing the right amount of this and that, and made by hand, from whisking eggs to mashing vegetables to making soup.

I wandered up the hill, taking some tulips with me from the garden, and knocked at Claudette's door. 'Come in,' she called. The door is always open throughout the day. 'These knees don't need to get up too many times,' she always says.

Another neighbour, Bénédicte, also an octogenarian, was there too, sitting in Claudette's kitchen. It was a warm afternoon but the oven was on as they had been baking together. A terracotta pie dish sat on top of the oven, its pastry shiny and golden, and the sharp aroma of hot rhubarb filled the air. Both women had a tiny glass of red wine in front of them on the table. Claudette poured me some of the ruby-red liquid from a stone bottle. I can't tell you how thankful I was at the thimble-sized glass – the homemade hooch almost stripped the skin off my tongue.

'I'm off to Carcassonne in the morning,' I said to them both. 'Raincoat or not?' Even though Claudette has no desire to go travelling herself, she likes to hear about the different places I visit and get a foreigner's view of things. I spend quite a bit of time visiting the four corners of France these days. Some of my French friends say I probably know their country better than they do, and that I see places differently, I suppose because I'm seeing these places for the first time, but also because I research the history and anecdotes of a place.

We then moved on to talking about the mobile shops. The Fish Man drives around the Seven Valleys from village to village for three days a week; the rest of the time he is at local markets and sourcing fish for his mobile fishmonger van. He reaches us on Tuesday mornings. He pulls up outside his regular customers' houses, hops into the back of the van, opens a side-panel window, pushes up a blue and white striped awning and voilà, the shop is open. Mussels from Boulogne-sur-Mer, crabs and crevettes, shrimps, coquilles Saint-Jacques and oysters are all displayed just as they would be in a shop. His arrival is the signal for the local cats to come lurking in numbers. The old farmer who owns the white horses often buys a tray of old bits of fish, which some people put in a soup but he gives to the local stray cats. I once saw more than twenty of them all meowing excitedly in his courtyard on a Tuesday morning as we walked past with the dogs.

The Meat Man comes on Wednesday and the Dairy, Spices and Bottles Man comes on Friday. He sells yoghurts and milk, shampoo and turmeric – anything and everything – and if you ask nicely for something he doesn't usually have, such as teabags, he'll get it in specially for you.

That day's main topic under discussion was the new Bread Man. I would normally hang a bag out on the gate and the old Bread Man would pop the bread in – occasionally with a recipe he thought might help my cooking skills – so I would not always see him. The new Bread Man, however, likes to chat. He looks like a short, melancholy Super Mario with a drooping moustache and deep brown eyes under a blue cap. 'He burns his *boulots* a bit too often for my liking,' said Bénédicte (in case you're wondering, a *boulot* is a large loaf). 'His baguettes are good, nice and crispy. His cakes are good too,' added Claudette. 'Those little *financiers* he brings are delicious. Madame Bernadette said they are the best she's ever had, apart from mine. But yes, I agree, his *boulots* are *merde*.'

'He likes a drink you know,' Bénédicte said as she lifted her own thimbleful of poison with shaky hands. She closed one eye and looked around as if he might suddenly appear in the room and demand a bottle of wine. This is how rumours begin in French villages. One person says something to someone else: it could be completely and utterly untrue, but if someone says it out loud then everyone agrees. After all, there is no smoke without fire.

'How do you know?' asked Claudette

'I can tell,' said Bénédicte, 'because he has the same colour nose as my Anton used to have and he liked a drink.'

'*Tac tac tac*,' said Claudette, sounding like a robot with a speech impediment.

What, you might ask, is that all about? It's something that French people say a lot. '*Tac tac tac*' comes from the word *d'accord*, which means okay and is used to show you understand or agree with something that's been said. It's hard to get right. I've tried saying it and I just get strange looks. It's the same when I say *cidre* (cider) – somehow the tiniest nuance in the pronunciation renders me unfathomable to French speakers. Sometimes instead of *tac tac tac*, they will say *tac tac*, or just *d'acc*, or even *dac-o-dac*.

Bénédicte and Claudette are full of pearls of wisdom about people's personalities and foibles. We get through postmen and women at a rate of knots in these parts. I have no idea why – perhaps they rotate them – but every new postie will be discussed and catalogued in this way. Recently we had a post lady with glasses as thick as the bottom of a wine bottle and jet-black hair that didn't quite match her wrinkled complexion. 'I bet she has a terrible temper. Look at that hair – dark hair, dark mood.' The poor woman probably never said boo to a goose, even though in our street there is obviously ample opportunity to do so, since Madame Jupe regularly leaves the gate of her pen open and all of her birds just wander about in the street.

One postman was apparently a potential serial killer because his 'eyes are too close together'. When the Fish Man went on holiday, his rounds were taken on by his brother, who came from Le Havre in Normandy to help out. 'You could tell he can't be trusted because he's got big earlobes,' Bénédicte commented.

'Is that your doggy?' asked the chatty new Bread Man one Tuesday, after he tooted the horn so much outside the house that I gave up trying to work and went out there. 'Yes, he is very friendly,' I said, looking down at Churchill, who had been in the pigsty with me while Ella and Bruno, who are totally in love at the moment, were in the back garden together. They have been leaving Churchill out a fair bit lately and he stands at the gate looking forlorn and pitiful. He loves to meet people and took an instant shine to the new Bread Man, chasing his own tail, running around and around in circles like a complete maniac.

He's learning English apparently (the Bread Man, not Churchill). He told me that his daughter was having English lessons at school and he was helping with her homework. He was hoping to practise on me, the only Brit, apart from Mark, in the village. And I think he might have swotted up for the Thursday delivery.

'The rain is very falling,' he said carefully. 'It like a river.' He tapped the side of his nose as if he had made this personal discovery while driving around in his little white van full of delicious-smelling bread. He wasn't wrong: a river of rainwater was cascading down the hill. I think it might have even been possible to surf it, though I wasn't tempted to try.

The next baguette delivery led to another English language lesson in the rain with the Bread Man:

'Where is your doggy? The rain has carried him?' He laughed at his own wit and his moustache wriggled as it if was trying to escape.

'The dog refuses to leave the pigsty,' I said. 'He doesn't like the rain.'

The Bread Man looked lost. 'What is pigsty?' I had no idea what the word is in French.

'The house where the pigs live,' I said.

'You have pigs living in your house?' He was incredulous.

'No. We have a small building in the garden where the pigs used to live. Now it is where I write.'

'You write with the pigs?'

In the end he drove off because Madame Bernadette, his next customer, was waving from the bottom of the hill for her bread. He was obviously running late.

I am pretty sure he will spread the word that the crazy Brit in the village has pigs in her house and they help with her writing. I'm not sure if that's worse than being known as Madame Merde.

Returning to the topic of the weather, Claudette assured me that locally we were in for good weather for the next few days – no raincoat needed the next morning at least.

Whenever I take a trip out of the region, I always go by train. In my little rural corner of France there's no public transport for miles so I have to drive to the town of Étaples-Le Touquet to take the train to Paris, from where you can travel all over France and beyond. It's not a speedy service to Paris, which is about the same distance away as London (approximately 150 miles). In fact, it's quicker to go to London, which takes less than 2.5 hours from my door to King's Cross St Pancras if I hop on the Eurostar at Calais, and that includes an hour driving to the station and going through customs.

I love the French rail network despite some strange rules linked to using the trains. For instance, it's illegal to carry a live snail on a French highspeed train – unless you have bought it a ticket. Any domesticated animal under 5 kg must be paid for, so when a traveller carrying a box of snails was stopped by a ticket inspector, a fine was applied (although the authorities did subsequently relent and reimburse the traveller). It's also illegal to kiss on the platform if the train has arrived – apparently this is to make sure that the passionate French don't cause delays. On the whole, after the UK, I find French trains refreshingly clean and comfortable; the people who work on them take real pride in their jobs; and the trains are almost always on time. Except when there are strikes.

France has a passion for striking. It's a serious subject and has its roots in the French Revolution of 1789 when people took to the streets, stormed buildings and overthrew the ruling royal family, proving to themselves that if they worked together they could change their world. Many countries simply don't have a strike culture and don't understand the importance that French people attach to their right to protest. Here, it is a way of life, just as much as eating cheese and drinking wine, and even those inconvenienced by strike action often accept it with little grumbling. There's even a website dedicated to who's striking and where, which is helpful if you're a travel writer who needs to travel round France by train.

Luckily there were no train strikes the next morning despite SNCF (Société nationale des chemins de fer français, the national state-owned railway company) being one of the most strike-hit services I have ever experienced. They have had a strike every year since 1947. Having left behind Pas-de-Calais, which was sunny just as Claudette had predicted, I arrived in Carcassonne where it was warm but overcast. I checked into my B&B at the base of the stunning citadel, with its turreted ramparts enclosing the city perched on a hill, and phoned Mark to let him know I'd arrived safely. 'How are things at home?' I asked. 'Dogs all right? Cats okay? You all right?'

'We're all okay, but there are more of us now than when you left,' said Mark. 'Another thirteen ducklings hatched this morning …'

The first rule of Wood Club is you don't talk about Wood Club

THE START OF June brought the sun and I saw my neighbours dragging dusty barbecues out of barns and sheds, ready for a weekend of outdoor feasting. Winston was in his usual spot under a lilac tree. He prefers to be alone but, inevitably, Shadow and Loulou will join him. Fat Cat isn't tolerated because he always ends up squashing everyone. 'Enry Cooper likes to sit on the wall in the front garden so he can watch the tractors go by. He loves it when the post van stops for parcel deliveries and the postie has to get out instead of leaning out the window to push papers through the post box. This is the cue for 'Enry Cooper to jump down and make friends. He adores people and will follow someone he likes for a long time before giving up and coming back home to be fed.

It was perfect weather for the annual Route des Vacances festival. The event harks back to the post-war days of summer when pasty-faced miners would bundle their families into vehicles of all sorts to make their way from the mining basin of Lens in Nord, leaving the now UNESCO-listed slag heaps behind to breathe in the fresh air at the seaside town of Berck-sur-Mer in Pas-de-Calais. Here, the owners of the coalmines also owned a large hotel where the miners could stay. Although it wasn't much more than 100 km away, the cars were slower than they are now and the journey was part of the holiday, spread out over a number of hours with stop-offs en route at towns such as Hesdin and Montreuil-sur-Mer. In memory of those days, and with the locals' everlasting love of tradition and heritage, a procession of vintage cars has followed in the tracks of the old miners' holiday route and has taken place annually for several years.

People come from miles around to admire the vintage vehicles parked on the main square in Hesdin, in front of the imposing sixteenth-century town hall. You don't have to be a petrolhead to appreciate the sight of row upon row of ancient cars, including the much-loved 2CVs, Renault Estafette vans and antiquated buses that look like they drove straight off a St Trinian's film set. Around 350 cars and a thousand people make the journey, many dressed appropriately for the occasion. Thousands of people turn up to look at the cars, remember the good old days and enjoy a knees-up in the town. If you ever need convincing that authentic France still exists, you'll find the evidence on the day the convoy comes to town.

'Built to carry a basket of eggs across ploughed fields and not make an omelette,' an old man was explaining to a little boy who was staring at a dusky blue 2CV, affectionately known as '*deux chevaux*' or '*la deudeuche*'. Despite the fact that these legendary lollopy cars haven't been made since 1990, there are still plenty of them about. Perhaps they were so popular as they really were a 'car of the people', and everyone in France knows someone who had one. They were cheap, simple and they just kept going. Not only was the suspension good enough that eggs on the back seat didn't break, but they were also able to accommodate a passenger wearing a hat – important for those Sunday church outings, and the seats were detachable for picnics!

The cafés in the town were doing a roaring trade despite it being a Sunday, when normally everything is closed. In the Café Le Commerce, which looks like it might have been delivered direct from the 1970s to its corner spot, tables and chairs spilled out onto the pavement, and we sat there taking in the spectacle of people enjoying a sunny day looking at cars.

After lunch the drivers returned to the square, ready to join a convoy to the seaside. The 2CV we had been admiring was fired up, its flat twin-cylinder engine sounding like no other car in the world. With a dashboard-mounted pull in, out and turn gearstick, it's an unusual drive to say the least. The procession departed in a slow and steady manner to continue its travels on largely empty roads all the way to the sea. Other car drivers beeped their hooters in appreciation as they passed, and all along the route people came out of their houses to wave and take photos.

The good weather felt like it was here to stay, so when Annette offered to look after the animals so we could have a day off to enjoy the sunshine, we jumped at the chance and decided to drive to Normandy for the day. Autoroutes stretch across the country, making it easy to get around once you reach them. Although it feels as if our little village is in the middle of nowhere, the A16 motorway can be reached in just twenty-five minutes and from there, Rouen, the historic capital of Normandy, is just an hour and a half away.

We hadn't been back to Normandy since taking my dad in June 2009 when we were still living in London. He had desperately wanted to be there for the sixty-fifth anniversary of D-Day. Aged sixty-eight at the time, he decided there were a few things he really wanted to do before he got too old, and being in Normandy for the D-Day remembrance ceremonies was one of them. On such a big occasion, and with dad only deciding at the last moment that he absolutely wanted to go more than anything else in the world (he wasn't a planner and sprung this bucket-list item on me at the last minute), it wasn't easy to get accommodation, so we ended up being an hour's drive from the main sites. For several days we drove back and forth to ceremonies and events. We watched a fly-past, chatted to veterans, went to some of the iconic sites such as Sainte-Mère-Église and Pegasus Bridge, and to cafés where veterans congregated and held listeners enthralled with their tales. We also visited the American cemetery, and it was only the second time in my whole life that I saw my dad cry (the other time was when my mum died). He was completely overwhelmed by the sight of the pristine grave markers, row upon row upon row. It didn't stop him moaning about the drive though, and when I suggested we add on a trip to Mont Saint-Michel he was adamant another hour's drive in the car was just too much. We took him anyway.

Mont Saint-Michel is majestic. It's one of those places where the magic shines through despite its wiggly cobbled streets being covered by tourists (around 2.5 million a year). It's a tiny town on a granite island cradled between the coasts of Brittany and Normandy. Lopsided half-timbered houses wind their way round what looks like an upside-down ice-cream cone, topped by a gravity-defying golden statue of Saint Michael. Victor Hugo, the great French writer, called it 'the pyramid of the seas' and you can really see what he meant. It's one of the wonders of the world and has attracted hordes of tourists since the Middle Ages.

I remember that when we wandered with Dad through the stone arch that forms the entry to the town, he stood there open-mouthed. Afterwards, we made our way up a cobbled hill and past chapels, souvenir shops and cafés in medieval buildings. We peered into the restaurant Mère Poulard, famous for its fluffy omelettes made to the same secret recipe since 1888, and cooked on an open fire in front of customers who have included Ernest Hemingway and Marilyn Monroe. We wandered down tiny alleyways and lost ourselves in the wonder of the ancient architecture. 'This,' said Dad, 'is one of those places that everyone ought to see before they die.'

The three of us stopped in a restaurant to have lunch. From the outside, it didn't look special, but it had a terrace overlooking the bay and we could see for miles. Far below us there were people armed with buckets, undertaking the great French tradition of *pêche à pied*, fishing by foot. 'It's not real fishing, is it?' Dad said. He prided himself on being a bit of an angler. His friends tell me he once went fishing at a lake in Kent and stopped to buy some bait on the way. Not liking what was on offer, he bought what was said to be a dead piranha, a small one, around a pound in weight, from a pet shop instead. He chucked it into the lake on the end of his rod where it promptly fell off and floated on the surface out of reach, causing much laughter among the anglers that day. A little while later a newspaper story appeared with a wild headline that a man had caught a piranha in the lake. It had, according to the report, dragged his line about 500 yards and took fifteen minutes to reel in, all 1 lb of it.

Normandy has its own feel and its own food. And if you go to Normandy, you had better like butter. And cheese. And garlic … Let's just say, don't go there if you're on a diet. Steaming bowls of mussels, fresh as can be, were put on the table before us with a basket filled with chunks of baguette for mopping up the creamy, garlicky sauce. Crispy fries and a green salad accompanied the fishy feast. Afterwards a selection of cheeses was brought to the table. I explained to Dad that it was polite to ask for up to three of the cheeses on show and the server would then cut a sliver of each for you. Of course, that didn't happen. Confronted with the sight of several cheeses, a ripe Brie and smelly Camembert, Livarot and pungent Pont l'Evêque, heart-shaped Neufchâtel and Pavé d'Auge, Dad had no idea which to choose.

'This one,' said the waiter, 'comes from a dairy farm in a sleepy village among the rolling hills. And this is one of the most creamy and delectable cheeses in the world … flavoured with a little Calvados, this one tastes of heaven, it's funky and delicious …' He rolled his tongue around the words, filtering them through his droopy moustache, proudly paying tribute to the local cheeses much like a sommelier does when describing wine.

'I'll have a bit of everything,' said Dad firmly. The waiter sliced expertly and popped the portions on a plate. Dad spread them over chunks of baguette and sighed happily as he took his first bite. He didn't share and he didn't stop until he had finished. 'I have eaten myself into a sitting position,' he announced, so we left him to enjoy the views and entertain some American tourists on the table next to ours. Dad was a great raconteur and loved to tell tall tales. I still don't know if the piranha story is true.

We went off to climb to the top of the Mont to visit the abbey at the summit of a steep stone staircase. It was far less crowded than the streets, which is not a surprise since there's no lift to the top so you really don't have a choice but to tackle a whopping 350 steps. There were a couple of paramedics sitting on a bench halfway up and we joked to each other that they must be there to help those who have eaten too much cheese to make it to the top without collapsing. Getting to the peak was worth every challenging moment of the climb. The thick stone walls of the abbey are punctuated with arched windows, which allow panoramic views over one of the most beautiful bays in the world. Inside the Gothic abbey there is a feeling of spirituality and of peacefulness, and you stop in wonder at cloisters that seem to be suspended halfway to heaven. The history of this place goes back millennia but it was in AD 708 that Aubert, the bishop of Avranches, dreamed he had an encounter with the archangel Michael, who instructed him to build a church on the island. Three times the archangel instructed the bishop, until finally, according to legend, he burnt a hole in the bishop's skull to drive home the message. Aubert built his chapel and the current abbey has stood on the same site since the eleventh century. As Mark said to me afterwards, it was one of those places you will always remember visiting for the first time.

Driving round the bay later, we stopped to watch the *pêcheurs à pied*, just like those foot fishermen we had seen from the ramparts of Mont Saint-Michel. We took off our shoes, rolled up our trousers and wandered onto the sandy beach. There were several groups of people bent over, scanning the ground, some gently scratching at the sand with rakes.

'Ask them what they're looking for,' urged Dad at the top of his voice in English. He couldn't speak French, but believed that saying things really loudly would help French people to understand him. An elderly woman who had been bent over, scanning the sand, looked up at us quizzically. She had a wrinkled face and a big smile underneath her wide-brimmed straw hat. She explained that she was seventy-five years old and was there with her family hunting for clams, winkles, cockles and whelks.

'You have to be careful not to catch too much,' she said. 'It would be bad for the fish to take too many and, besides, the gendarmes might check.' She explained that the amount you can take is strictly regulated and fines are steep if you overfish. 'We depended on fish to live when I was young,' she told us. 'Of course, life's not so hard now, but it's good to catch what you can for free, *non*?' She covered her bucket with seaweed. 'You must be cunning like a rat and have plenty of patience, but the prize is the freshest fish you've ever tasted.' She stooped to pluck a shell from the sand and dropped it into her bucket. *'Mangez bien, riez souvent, aimez beaucoup.'* She winked and wandered off to find more fish. I explained to Dad that she had said, 'Eat well, laugh often, love abundantly.' A perfect philosophy for life.

Going back to Normandy for the first time without Dad was going to be a bittersweet experience. We decided to go to places we had not visited with him and, although there's plenty of choice, number one on my to-do list for some time had been to visit the house and garden of Claude Monet in Giverny. We left at dawn, leaving Annette to feed the animals, and arrived in time to be the first into the gardens, which we had to ourselves for a while. There are some places that don't live up to all the hype – Monet's garden is the complete opposite. It surpassed my expectations. Inside the house, it feels just as if the great artist has popped out to take a wander round the flowerbeds or collect eggs from the chickens. Copies of his paintings hang in the rooms, and vases of flowers scent the air. His bedroom window was thrown open to reveal the glory of the garden and, as I stood there looking out, I could see why he was so obsessed with colours.

By the time we got home late that night, four more ducklings had hatched. By now I was starting to worry that we were going to be overrun as there were still five ducks nesting. I knew we wouldn't be able to keep them all and finding homes in which they would be pets and not dinner wasn't going to be easy. But I had to start somewhere and put out the word that there were ducks going free to those who wanted a pet. My first takers lived close by – a British couple who were vegetarians and had a big house with a pond. We took Delilah, Fenella and Henri, who dived into the pond as soon as we arrived, taking to their new home like ... well, ducks to water.

'Can we call them different names?' asked the woman. 'He looks like a Bill to me.' I knew that the ducks would be fine there. A week later, however, their new owners were on the phone asking if we could come and get Bill. 'He's rocket-fuelled with the ladies,' they said. 'We love him, he's super friendly and eats out of our hands already, but he's incredibly frisky. All our ducks are now sitting on eggs!'

We found a few more homes for the girls but no one wanted males. It seems everyone except me knew just how randy ducks are! In the meantime, I had gone into Sherlock Holmes mode in my search for new eggs to make sure no more new nesting took place. I offered the eggs to my neighbours and friends and had a good take-up rate. Everyone knew that duck eggs are fabulous for making all sorts of dishes from creamy custard to rich ice cream and golden omelettes.

I took some eggs to Annette and on the way home stopped off in the village of Hesmond at a farm run by a woman known to locals as 'the goat lady', though her real name is Valerie. She was making cheese when I got there and invited me to join her. Before we could start, the goats needed milking.

'The first milk is always for the cat,' she said as she milked with ease, and on cue a fluffy grey cat appeared from nowhere and began lapping up the warm milk from a small dish, licking her lips greedily afterwards. Then it was my turn to have a go at milking. I have to tell you, some goats will look you right in the eye when you approach them, and it's not always a friendly look. Milking a goat is not as easy as you might think; they are fidgety creatures and easily distracted, and they were quite happy to wander off while I was still hanging on to them.

Afterwards, we donned Smurf-blue-coloured plastic slippers, white lab jackets and hideous hairnets that made us both look quite demented before racing to her tiny cheese-preparation room. Valerie is always in a hurry and rushes everywhere. I had to run to keep up with her.

'It's best to use the milk when it's really fresh,' she explained as she showed me what to do. Everything was done by hand. No fancy equipment, just hard work and expertise. We squeezed and groped curds, we poured and stirred, topped up moulds, turned the older moulds over and rubbed some salt on some of them in their tins, which were heart-shaped, round or pyramid style.

I have eaten a lot of cheese in my time, but I have never had cheese quite like Valerie's. The locals say she has a secret ingredient – passion – and I'm sure they are right. My reward for helping out was a round of an intoxicatingly tangy cheese, covered in fresh herbs and edible petals.

As we progressed through June, the first set of ducklings were growing fast and had become quite delinquent. They frequently escaped from the pen, had learned to climb trees and were happy to eat everything in the garden. I had taken to covering all the vegetable beds with twigs to keep them off. There's no other word for it – it was mayhem. They watched the older ducks pecking at my boots and jumping into the food buckets I carried down to the bottom of the garden, and they all followed suit.

In all the time we had kept chickens we'd never had a chicken egg hatch, so we started to think it would never happen. Our girls are all far too lazy, we thought. But that month, everything changed. Tallulah Pompom Head (she has a fluffy feathered hairdo) sat on eggs in a bucket and Joan Crawford would hardly come out of the coop – she was seriously obsessed.

Claudette added warnings to the ones Jean-Claude had been giving us for a while now. 'You need to get control of this garden,' she counselled, adding that one male duck and ten female ducks could easily become many, many more in just a year. She leaned over the fence and surveyed the birds, who were clearly ruling the roost. She had bird problems, too – her goose had escaped and, finding rich pickings in the hedgerows in the road in front of her house, was reluctant to come back home. After I'd chased it in and Claudette shut the gate on it, we stopped in her ever-hot kitchen for a tiny glass of wine. Even worse than usual, it tasted like it was made in a smelly old bucket at the bottom of a thousand-year-old well. But I always drink it.

Claudette loves to talk, especially about anything to do with the Queen. I told her about visiting my nan, who lived near Windsor when I was a kid, and the polo matches to which she would sometimes take me. I remembered, when I was eleven, Prince Charles gave me a polo ball and I just stood open-mouthed like a total idiot, unable to speak. And the time I was sitting in a square near St Paul's Cathedral on my lunchbreak, when a Rolls-Royce pulled up and the Queen hopped out and disappeared into a nearby sweetshop!

I made my visit to Claudette shorter than usual as I had to go to church. There is an enormous eighteenth-century church in the village, which harks back to the days when there were many more inhabitants and everyone went to church. A tall Gothic-looking building with a black slate roof and colourful stained-glass windows, it looks abandoned and is only opened on the thankfully rare occasion of a funeral. When one does take place, a formal notice is dropped in all mailboxes so that people can go and pay their respects. In such a small village as this, as in so many in France, it's simply not economical or practical to hold services and heat the church on cold days. But among the usual weekly special-offer brochures had come a notice that, for one night only, the church would be opened to host a gospel choir from America and everyone in the village was invited.

Mark and I arrived early and, for once, so did everyone else. The church was absolutely packed. We sat perched on the thinnest pews ever, hundreds of years old and, I suspect, made like that to keep churchgoers from dozing off. There was no napping that night, that's for sure. A full-blown professional choir, beautifully dressed, with their state-of-the-art microphones and music mixers, filled the ancient church with their songs of hope and praise. It wouldn't have been any less strange if the Rolling Stones had taken a wrong turn on their way from London to Paris and pitched up at the town hall to perform. The audience sang, danced and applauded wildly. It was an uplifting night that didn't end when we all filed out of the church with broad grins on our faces.

In honour of such an illustrious visit, someone had laid on fireworks. Rockets were tied to some of the gravestones and pinged off across the rooftops, leaving a trail of colourful sparkles behind them. Bizarre for sure, but as someone said, a celebration of life among those departed. The next day, the church was closed again.

Summer had begun but, as expected in northern France, this also meant rain. It seemed that every conversation we had involved the weather (or Brexit, but I'm not going there). We talked about how much it was raining, and about getting caught in the rain; we wondered how much it might rain tomorrow, and sighed at how much it rained yesterday.

Jean-Claude popped by one particularly wet day that month and stood dripping in the hall as he took off his boots before coming into the kitchen for coffee and to chat to Mark.

'Let's talk wood,' he began.

'Huh?' said Mark.

'Wood, firewood. Do you have enough for winter?'

'Well, we've got some on order from the Wood Man at Azincourt, coming in July,' said Mark, wondering where this was leading.

'We wondered if you wanted to join our Wood Club,' said Jean-Claude. 'My *copain* [mate] is leaving the club – he's got too old and his son put central heating in for him – so there's a vacancy if you're interested.'

'I could be,' said Mark, though he didn't sound too sure. A former policeman, he's naturally suspicious. 'What do you do in the Wood Club?'

'For one week each year, we cut down damaged trees on Claudette's land, chop it up into firewood and stack it in the big barn behind the Parisians' house to season it.' Claudette is the biggest landowner in the village and has fields that cover quite a distance. 'Then we share out the seasoned wood from three years ago to the club members when it's just ripe for winter.'

He explained there were a total of six places in the club. He was the leader, of course, as Claudette is his *belle-maman*. Then there was Claude Sr, aka 'Claude at the top of the big hill'. He drives a skinny tractor, which is at least as ancient as he is, its once vibrant red paint a mere memory. His son Claude is known to all as 'Claude at the top of the small hill' and lives three farmhouses up from us. There is a big dip in between the two hills. Every day 'Claude at the top of the big hill' visits 'Claude at the top of the small hill' (I hope you're still with me) in his tractor. I can set my watch by the journey. Lunch starts precisely at noon as the tractor splutters down one hill and finishes precisely at 2 p.m. when it returns down the other hill. Little else moves outside during this sacred two-hour recess, except for Bernadette's chickens who forage under the hedgerows for their lunchtime treat. Apparently every first son and every first daughter in the family has been given the name Claude for two hundred years.

Petit Frère was also a member, as well as Monsieur Durand and Monsieur Rohart, both former farmers. Jean-Claude made getting into the club sound as if it was an exclusive and coveted achievement. And he told Mark, with a big smile, that all the members agreed it was time for new blood and thought Mark would be ideal. 'Claudette's land is kept tidy and we get wood to use for ourselves – it's a *gagnant-gagnant*, a win-win,' he said. We were honoured to be included (well, Mark, rather than me – it's men only, much like the hunting club. But I could go without being a lumberjack for a week).

This being France, Mark was invited to meet everyone – even though he knew them all already – at a formal meeting in Jean-Claude's garage. He arrived at Jean-Claude's house at the appointed time and knocked at the door – there was no answer. He knocked again, loudly, and heard the creaking of the up-and-over garage door being lifted. Jean-Claude stuck his head out and beckoned Mark in. We've both spent plenty of time in there at parties hastily moved inside along with the barbecue, sound system, chairs and tables when it rains, but today there was just one small plastic table and six chairs. Mark was asked to sit down and Petit Frère dished out bottles of beer.

'Right,' said Jean-Claude, 'we need to set the date for the Wood Club to convene this year. Is everyone free next week?' Round the table everyone pulled small diaries from their pockets, except for Mark.

'Hmm,' said Monsieur Durand, 'no good for me. I've got a doctor's appointment.' Monsieur Rohart had an optician's appointment and Petit Frère had to go to the chiropodist. 'I've got my annual check-up that week,' said Claude Sr.

'Last week of June then?' said Jean-Claude.

The old men turned the pages of their diaries and miraculously were all free of medical appointments that week. They turned to Mark, who told me later he was tempted to come up with an excuse just for fun, but thought better of it. Later Jean-Claude told him they always do the woodcutting in the last week of June (whatever the pretence of checking other dates) and to make sure he kept it free in the diary he doesn't have.

It never ceases to amaze me that, although French people never arrive when they say will, drive like maniacs because they are always late and hardly start anything on time, the administration and planning of events is a national obsession. Even train strikes are planned to a timetable days in advance and nearly always logged on the SNCF website the night before so that travellers can plan around the strikes.

The rest of the meeting was largely unrelated to wood, but Mark was told that he shouldn't share details of what they do with anyone else, or they would all want to be included.

On the morning the Wood Club was due to convene, Mark presented himself at the *longère* barn as instructed and Jean-Claude showed him the barns where the three-year-old wood was stacked. He estimated there was enough for everyone to have around 10 tons and the first job was to deliver it by tractor so the barn was freed up for the new wood to be cut.

Jean-Claude's trailer was first to be filled. Mark was paired with Petit Frère, who works as a part-time tractor mechanic and is as strong as a small ox. Jean-Claude sat in the cab of the tractor, directing and making sure the tractor was 'properly loaded' before taking his allowance up to Claudette's house to be stored in her barn. While this was being done, Claude Sr's tractor was loaded by the other team who, despite clearly competing with Mark and Petit Frère, couldn't keep up with the younger duo, who were working on Claudette's own allocation.

Three hours later, they stopped for lunch at Claudette's, each removing their boots before entering her spotless kitchen in their socks. As is the law in France, they stopped for two hours. Okay, it's not the law, but it often feels like it is. Claudette served French onion soup, thick with melting cheese, and crusty baguettes, as they all teased Jean-Claude about sitting in the tractor instead of helping. '*Non, non,*' he said, 'my heart, I have to be careful.' Petit Frère said he's been saying the same thing since they were both young.

Claudette dished up a pile of buttery fondant potatoes with a green salad from her garden and *rôti de porc au lait*, pork roasted in milk, and finally a *tarte Tatin aux abricots*, all washed down with a bottle of wine (thankfully not the deadly homemade stuff). Mark said he could quite easily have gone to sleep all afternoon after that. But the Wood Club had to finish emptying the barn by lunchtime the next day or they would run out of time. The men lifted, loaded and delivered all afternoon, and the next morning our wood was dropped in the front garden ready for us to stack.

The next day's lunch was at the home of Monsieur Durant, as Petit Frère was single, Claude Sr was a widower and Monsieur Rohart's wife was at her mother's house in Cassel, a pretty little town on top of a hill in the far north. I did offer to cook in the evening but, as the whole village knows, I can't cook that well so I was told that a barbecue on a Saturday night in July or August would work for everyone, as they were sure to be too tired after the long hard days of being woodcutters.

Mark told me that Madame Durant served an equally expansive lunch of mackerel in white wine followed by a steaming bowl of *poule au pot*, a chicken stew (said to have its origins in the sixteenth century when King Henri IV of France allegedly said that he would ensure that 'every Frenchman should be able to have a hen in his pot on a Sunday' at a time when poor people rarely ate meat). This was followed with a melt-in-your-mouth chocolate tart. That afternoon, the Wood Club visited the fields and made notes about which trees would be cut and where new ones would be planted. It is a system that has worked well for years.

On the third day, the chopping began in earnest. Petit Frère wielded a chainsaw almost as tall as him. Cutting large wedges into the bottom of the chosen trees, he was covered in woodchips and, with seeming indifference, leaned against the trees to make them crash down exactly where he wanted them. Then they chopped the tall trees into smaller pieces with a saw attached to the back of Jean-Claude's tractor, and stacked them into the trailers to go to the barn.

As Madame Rohart was back from her mother's she provided lunch that day. Mark came home and described it to me in great detail: mushrooms and girolles fried in butter, white wine and cream with garlic served on toasted slices of brioche, beef cooked in beer with herbs, and a heavenly crème caramel. I was starting to feel envious of Wood Club.

On the fourth day, the men chopped, loaded, unloaded and stacked, with a short break when Bernadette came home from work with freshly baked baguettes, cheese, ham and pâté. As the last day loomed, apparently the mood had changed somewhat. The men were tired and just wanted to get the work finished. There was no long lunch that day. When Mark returned home, he admitted that although he was happy to be involved in his first village club, he was pretty sure it would be easier just to buy wood and have it delivered.

All hail – it's a disaster

THE WEATHER IN northern France can be mixed in July, but we were on the home run with the shutters and the painting of the house. Although there was a time when I thought we would never ever be finished, it did feel like maybe, just maybe, we were beginning to see light at the end of the tunnel. Bit by bit, the neglected old house was starting to look like the beauty I always dreamed it could be. We joked that by the time we actually finished, we'd have to start all over again. But we felt optimistic, and the finish line was in sight.

At least, that's what we thought. But fate had other plans. On the 6 July, at six minutes before 6 p.m. (a detail I will never forget), a freak hailstorm hit our tiny area of the Seven Valleys.

We were driving home that afternoon in our van from the seaside town of Berck-sur-Mer on the Opal Coast, where we had been shopping. It had been a very sunny day, and the whole of the first week of July had been wonderfully hot. We'd spent the afternoon in Berck, an unpretentious, friendly and authentic seaside town. It was once a fishing village but thanks to its iodized climate, it gained a reputation as a place for recuperation for the sick and infirm to the point where, in 1869, a hospital was inaugurated there by Empress Eugénie, wife of Napoleon III. The town still retains an air of faded grandeur, though the hospital is being converted to apartments and a hotel. The sandy beach is perfect for picnics and kite flying, and a world-famous annual kite championship is held there. There's also an irresistible sweetshop where they make boiled sweets in front of you and, once tasted, you'll never forget them. The Pas-de-Calais department isn't usually on the bucket list for those who seek grand chateaux and sumptuous tourist sites – it's something of a hidden gem and requires a bit of time to explore.

The main entry point to France, Calais processes more than 10 million passengers a year from the UK. Arriving in their droves, the vast majority follow the *autres directions* sign straight out of town and onto the autoroute to somewhere else. They look neither right nor left, oblivious to the rich heritage to be found in ancient towns and villages, and utterly unaware of the marvellous bistros, cafés, traditional *estaminets* (Flemish inns) and some of the finest gastronomic restaurants in France.

As we approached our turn-off, the sky started to turn an ominous dark grey. When we left the main road to go down the hill that leads to our village, small balls of ice began to fall, hitting the van with a loud ping. Within seconds, a sea of white hailstones covered the road. The intensity of the storm increased incredibly quickly, and Mark pulled the van over to the side of the road as it became difficult to see where we were going.

It was an amazing sight and, fascinated, I started to film it on my mobile phone. The hailstones seemed to get bigger and bigger. They were the size of tennis balls by now, and the noise became deafening. Thwack, thwack, thwack as they smashed onto the van. My fascination began to be replaced by fear – I'd never seen anything like it, and we suddenly felt quite vulnerable in our little van.

'Cover your eyes,' shouted Mark as the front window started to crack. Suddenly it caved in, spewing tiny shards of glass into the van. Even though I was terrified, I carried on filming. I'm not sure why, perhaps because it was so staggeringly awful and I wasn't able to turn away. A car sped past us, as if trying to rush through the storm. One of its wing mirrors was hanging down, bouncing against the passenger door. We watched the car in horror as it slid about over the huge ice balls.

The deluge went on for just under six minutes according to the video on my phone. Then, just as suddenly as it had started, it stopped. We got out of the van and brushed the glass from our clothes, looking around us in disbelief. The van was covered in massive dents as if someone had been throwing bricks at it. The wing mirrors were hanging off, the windscreen was in bits.

We hadn't really been able to talk to each other while the storm was going on as the crashing and banging of the huge nuggets of solid ice pounding the metal had been so immense. Now it began to rain, and the downpour was torrential. We got back in the van and Mark turned the key in the ignition. Thankfully the van started. We drove slowly down the hill, peering through the caved-in windscreen and bumping over a river of hailstones, which were now being carried by the rainwater. Our home was just two minutes away and as I began to recover from the shock of what had just happened, a gnawing pain in my stomach started as I wondered what awaited us. The journey felt a lot longer than two minutes.

As we drove past the first house on the outskirts of the village, the old mayor's house, we slowed down to take a good look. We were relieved to see that it seemed fine, apart from a garden full of white hailstones. It is a modern house with a shiny tiled roof and garage. It was almost as if nothing had happened.

But as we drove on, we realized that it was the only house that had survived the storm unscathed. We passed twenty more buildings before we got to our own and they had all shared a similar fate. The old tiled roofs were in a terrible state, as was the slate roof of the church along with some of its stained-glass windows. By the time we pulled into our garden, we were fearing the worst.

The six-minute tempest had destroyed our car sitting in the driveway. The roof of the house, with its lovely old handmade tiles, had clearly borne the brunt of the onslaught; it was peppered with holes. It looked as if every single tile had been damaged and many lay in pieces in the garden below. The new loft windows we had fitted were also smashed to pieces and the roofs of the pigsty and woodsheds had all but disintegrated.

We ran to the back of the house to check the animals. The dogs were thankfully under shelter in their little brick house with its new roof still intact. The cats were hiding unharmed under the terrace, and the triple-glazed plastic roof didn't have a mark on it. Even the birds were okay, hiding in the coops or cowering under the terrace with the cats. My beautiful greenhouse was a pile of broken glass and the vegetable patch was destroyed. Great chunks of ice lay everywhere.

Opening the front door of the house, we were confronted by the sight of water pouring through the ceiling of the hall and the sitting room. The roof was ruined and, with nothing to stop the rain, every room upstairs had terrible water damage.

I burst into tears, overcome by the carnage in front of us. Mark was much more practical. He declared that there was no time for crying, and pointed out that we needed to try to make the house watertight straight away in case it rained all through the night. But first, we needed to check on our neighbours.

We walked down the hill and could see people emerging from their houses, taking stock of their damaged roofs and looking around in disbelief at the disaster zone. Bernadette passed us as she drove home from work, to be met with Jean-Claude standing in their front garden, shaking his head in disbelief. Everyone seemed to be walking around like us in a state of stunned silence, checking on neighbours and wondering where to start. The new mayor arrived within minutes and took over the task of checking the houses and making sure the electricity cables that supply the village weren't damaged. Often when it's very windy, a tree will come down onto the lines and we'll all be plunged into darkness without phones until its fixed.

Despite the violence of the storm, the damage to life was less severe. We discovered that two cats had been killed, and one poor woman who was walking home from a neighbour's house was hit on the head by a hailstone and had to have seventeen stitches. And the electricity still worked.

When we were sure no one needed anything other than something to try and cover the roofs as best they could to protect against the still falling rain, Mark searched in the sheds for tarpaulins. Meanwhile, I phoned Annette to make sure she was okay. Her village is just a couple of miles away and, though it too had been hit by hailstones, the situation was nowhere near as bad as ours. As only a few tiles had been lost on their roof, Gary and Annette drove to our house as quickly as they could with all the tarpaulins they could muster. Arriving in our village, they said other places they passed en route showed signs of damage, but nothing like on the scale our village had experienced.

Gary and Mark clambered up on the roof, trying not to slide off in the rain, and tied down the plastic sheets across as much of the missing tiling as they could.

The rain abruptly stopped soon after and the sun came out. The hailstones melted. The birds sang in the trees. I thought of the words of the American poet Robert Frost:

'In three words I can sum up everything I have learned about life: it goes on.'

We slept fitfully that night and woke the next morning to the sound of major activity in the village. Several carpentry and roofing companies turned up with van loads of plastic sheeting to help cover roofs and to give repair estimates for people to send to their insurers so that the big clean-up could begin. The mayor went from house to house, checking that everyone was okay and letting the villagers know that he would be contacting the regional government to get the storm declared a natural disaster for insurance purposes, which would speed up the process of reimbursement and repair. Cherry pickers were out in force, lifting teams up to reach roofs throughout the village. In stark contrast to the day before, the sun stayed out all day, and it would have felt as if nothing had ever happened, except for the sight of buildings wrapped in plastic and the sound of builders shouting instructions and banging hammers.

That day we met the Parisians. The mayor had phoned them to let them know what had happened. He has contact details for everyone who lives here and, if you go on holiday, you can let him know and he'll make sure your house is regularly checked by Jean-François, the village handyman. We were standing on the corner of the little alleyway where the Parisians' house is tucked away from the main road, chatting to one of the builders about coming to give an estimate, when a car turned in. The driver stopped to lean out of the window. '*Merde*,' he said, 'this is bad, eh?'

'Awful,' I agreed. 'Are you the Parisians?' Of course, no French person would ask this. Although they have a reputation for being aloof as a nation, being forthright isn't considered particularly good manners. The author Peter Mayle once said that a neighbour had told him that it was unfortunate that he was English, but that most people outside of Paris preferred even the English to Parisians!

The woman who was sitting next to him got out of the car, came around to us and shook hands as she laughingly said, 'Is that what you call us here? Yes, we are the Parisians!' The man got out too and shook hands with Mark and me. 'They call us the British Ch'tis,' I said.

The Parisians certainly seemed friendly enough, though he with his Hermès scarf and she with her high-heeled ankle boots and elegant cropped trousers and jacket stood out like a sore thumb. They couldn't stop for long, they said, because they needed to see what damage had been done and make arrangements for any repairs, though from where we all stood we could see that their new roof had stood up to the onslaught pretty well. They told us that they wouldn't be back in July – he was a policeman and had to work weekends – but they would be spending August at their house and they invited us round for drinks.

Unlike the Parisians', 90 per cent of the houses in the village needed new roofs. All of the old houses, with the traditional-style thick terracotta tiles so popular in this area, had severe damage. Claudette, owner of the poshest house in the village, had lost most of her black slate tiles, the sort you get on chateaux and manor houses. All of the new tiled roofs had minimal damage.

I contacted our insurers and explained what had happened. I could tell they didn't believe me when I said our house, van and car had been destroyed by giant hailstones. Who could blame them? I sent them the video I'd taken. They called me back and said the assessor would visit us the following week. I never shared the video with anyone else because you can hear me rather dramatically saying 'I don't want to die' above the pounding of the hailstones.

For the next few days, newspaper reporters and cameramen turned up to cover the story of the biblical weather that had hit our little village. A few people had saved some of the hailstones in their freezers and posed for pictures holding the balls of ice, unsmiling as instructed. For the next few weeks, we were big news locally and people came from miles around to see for themselves what had taken place. Nothing like it had happened since weather records began.

The next week, the insurance man turned up. He had driven from Paris where, even there, they had heard of the storm in the 'North Pole' of France. He walked around the house and garden making copious notes on his clipboard, his face impassive. He looked over the two estimates we had received, one for 40,000 euros and one for 26,000 euros, to repair the roof at the front of the house, which had taken the brunt of the damage, and to the outbuildings.

He signed off on the cheapest quote, or at least the part that covered the main roof. As with everyone else whose vehicles were exposed during the storm, our car and van were deemed wrecks, too expensive to repair, so they were written off and we received money towards new cars – though not anywhere near as much as we had paid for them. The vehicles still worked, though, and we needed them to get around until everything was sorted out, so we got the windows repaired, and Mark, who is a former car mechanic among other things, sorted out the broken wing mirrors. In the end, we bought the vehicles back from the insurers and kept them, as did many of our neighbours. If you ever drive through a small village in the middle of nowhere and spot dozens of cars that look like they've been attacked by a club-wielding giant, you'll know where I live.

The roofs of the outbuildings were not covered by the insurance, nor was the greenhouse or anything in the garden. As the cost of a new roof was a third of what we had paid for the whole house, we were still very grateful.

The roofers said they couldn't start work until November. But with summer coming up, we knew how lucky we were. It seems that the entire building trade down tools in July and August and nothing changes for a storm. We didn't know it then, but some people would wait more than a year for the repair work to be done. We didn't complain about November but hoped it wouldn't be too wet a summer and it wouldn't snow early. Again, we were lucky – that summer was one of the warmest and driest ever in our region. It felt like the north was the new south.

For a while, our enthusiasm for renovation was dampened but at the same time we knew we'd been very fortunate. None of our animals was harmed, we were safe and the house could be repaired. It could have been far worse. And life went on.

Arya, one of my chickens, with a needle-like beak, turned up at the door with ten chicks the next week. They were beautiful yellow and black fluffy creatures that squeaked at the top of their voices. Arya then flew over the fence into our next-door neighbour's garden, leaving us to look after the kids. With several cats, both our own and strays living in local barns, we knew they needed protection and so we took them under our wing, popping them into a cage under a heat lamp in the house – much to the disgust of the cats, who took it in turns to stare at the interlopers.

Meanwhile, at three months old, Ken the abandoned cockerel had become decidedly odd. He took a bit of a dislike to any flowers that were blooming and pulled off their heads. Not only that, he had taken to terrorizing me – it was hard to feel at ease in the garden as he started to sit in the trees, lying in wait for me to pass by, when he would jump down and run around me, squawking aggressively. He had also started to throw himself at the windows when he saw me in the kitchen. I had never been stalked by a chicken before – it was unnerving.

And another duckling arrived. It had been abandoned and was prematurely born with hardly any feathers. It couldn't walk as it had very weak legs. I sat and held it for hours, keeping it company as I was fairly sure it wasn't going to survive. But when it made it through the first day, I popped it into the cage with the abandoned chicks. We gave it swimming lessons in the bathroom sink several times a day on the advice of a lady who saw a video I posted on Instagram and knew about keeping ducks. Over time, its legs strengthened. The chicks and the duckling played well together and eventually I moved them all into a nursery pen in the garden. To this day, they get along famously.

Quatorze Juillet is a national holiday. It's Bastille Day to us – but the French never call it that and think it odd that non-French people do. Coming so soon after the storm this year, it was an unusually quiet day in the village. So, we decided to head to Montreuil-sur-Mer where every Bastille Day (I can't help it, I'm British) sees the town stage a spectacular antiques market.

This little medieval town, with its upper part encircled by ancient ramparts, has seen its fair share of drama over the centuries. Once it lived up to its suffix 'sur-Mer': it was a thriving port town and the only royal harbour in the tenth century, but the water has long since retreated. It has been laid siege to, and was fortified by Louis XIV's military engineering genius Vauban, and it was Napoleon's choice of campsite when planning to invade England. It even inspired Victor Hugo to write *Les Misérables*, and was the HQ for Field Marshal Douglas Haig during the First World War. Outside the town's pretty theatre, you'll spot a statue of him looking very stern astride a horse, cast by the sculptor Paul Landowski, who created *Christ the Redeemer* in Rio.

These days it's rather quieter. But it still has ankle-busting, chest-thumping hills to climb if you're on foot, and its cobbled streets are lined with grand houses and ancient cottages, with the privileged few living in the upper town, of course. Those in the lower town were, to Hugo, *les misérables*. They have a saying here in France, '*Tenir le haut du pavé.*' It means to succeed in life, but its literal translation is to walk on the high side of the pavement, a term that dates back to the Middle Ages, when in towns such as Montreuil wastewater (and other things) were chucked onto the cobbled streets and ran down the hills. The streets were therefore built sloping into the middle so that the waste would run away from doors. If you were rich in those days, you could walk on the high side where it was cleaner. If you were poor, you had to walk in the middle. It's why when protestors in the French Revolution tore up cobblestones to throw at the authorities, it was more than pure vandalism – it was symbolic.

Enchanting streets such as rue du Clape en Bas, with its artisan shops and bars, and rue du Petit Coquempot, where archers shot birds for practice in the Middle Ages, have a quaint charm that makes the town a magnet for savvy Brits looking for somewhere deliciously French, but close to home. Montreuil, though small, calls itself a '*destination gastronomique*' and packs a big punch in terms of French cuisine. When it comes to wining and dining, the choice in the town is second to none.

We like to go to the bars where the locals go, like Le Victor Hugo where Madame has an automatic snack dispenser, perfect to go with aperitifs. When she first got the dispenser, it caused something of a stir and was talked about in villages for miles around. Another favourite is the skinny Café Vert in rue Pierre Ledent. Its slightly gone-to-seed décor offers a taste of a France that hasn't changed for years. Rickety old barstools teeter on a beer-stained floor and lean precariously against the tatty wooden bar. A dreadlocked barman and a barmaid who sometimes sports a pirate-like patch serve the locals, who cunningly avoid the barstools and sit on the uncomfortable benches and chairs at small wooden tables when not playing on the old Le Foot table. With hardly any room on the pavement outside, a couple of plastic garden chairs are squeezed up against the wall so that regulars can sit *à la terrasse* and watch the cars go by, clattering over the cobbles. It's friendly and authentic, and they make a robust kir.

These bars are not the reason that this place is a gastronomic wonderland. There's a superb Saturday morning market and the buzzing restaurant scene includes some serious players, with two-Michelin-star chef Alexandre Gauthier leading the way at his restaurant La Grenouillère. Parisians come here for a genteel country break and celebrities such as Hugh Grant are lured by its gourmet reputation. You can get the most delicious *flammekueche* at Le Caveau, a quintessential brasserie in the town square, and for nights when only a takeaway will do, there's even a terrific kebab shop, which in these parts is a rarity. Throw in Fromagerie Caseus (the shop that provided the cheese for our New Year's Eve spread) and Gremont, where they make delectable cakes and a huge loaf of bread named a Valjean (in honour of Monsieur Hugo), which you can buy by the slice, and you'll completely understand why a town with only around two thousand inhabitants is making gastronomic waves.

Although we were there for the antiques market that day, I couldn't resist buying a string of the most incredibly pungent smoked garlic. The aroma accompanied me from stall to stall, earning me a smile from sellers and a bit of extra bargaining power. The streets were flooded with happy families strolling and browsing for treasure, though I was under strict instructions from Mark not to buy anything too big as the town was closed to traffic for the antiques market and we had been forced to park outside the centre. We joined a trickle of people trudging up into the upper town, dragging behind them all manner of carts and trolleys to be filled – a veritable pilgrimage.

It's easy to get carried away here. There's something to suit all tastes and the prices often seem more reasonable if the goods are spread out over the sun-baked cobbles. Professional dealers and treasure hunters wander the streets, bartering and bargaining. If you're looking for a vintage top hat, a gorgeous armoire, a cast-iron Godin wood or coal fire, swish and swanky or battered and tatty – whatever type of antique you seek – you're likely to find it here alongside all manner of things. I don't think I've ever been to a flea market and not found something with which to fall in love, and the Montreuil antiques market is full of temptations.

I spotted an enormous clockface, possibly from a local clocktower, which was taller than Mark. 'Absolutely not,' said Mark hastily. 'I can't get that in the car or the van.' Next, a life-sized marble bust of a Marie Antoinette lookalike caught my attention. Mark rolled his eyes. The silver zinc 1930s wood oven got the same reaction. But when we got to a stall selling vintage cutlery, china, chef's hats, chef jackets, copper pans and tableware glinting in the sun – we were both hooked. It often feels like absolutely everyone we meet in France is either an excellent cook, a great cook or a good cook. Some of the dishes that my neighbours make wouldn't be out of place on a table in a fine restaurant in London. Even I have improved thanks to help from Constance, who on her visits from Lille will often invite me in to help her knead, bake, steam or mix something delicious.

The stallholder was portly and red-faced, sporting a toque with his chef's jacket undone (the buttons were never going to rendezvous). He sniffed the air as we looked over his stall. 'Mm, garlic,' he exclaimed. 'I see you have good taste. You are a cook, of course.'

'Erm no, I'm British and I'm learning to cook but I'm not very good. My friends here call me "flop chef, not top chef",' I said.

'*Oh, là là,*' he replied, pushing his hat back to take a better look at me. 'Have you tried cooking with the right tools? It really does help,' he said pointedly as he spread his arms wide over the stall to indicate his wares. Once a Frenchman starts to get carried away about his topic, it's hard to stop him. With chop-busting gusto, he began to wax lyrical about the great hotels and top restaurants he supplied, how his tableware could help to increase enjoyment because the food could look so good in it, how his copper pans were essential to make good jam and, importantly, that dressing the part made for better performance. A crowd gathered around us, old ladies nodding in agreement, leaning over to lift pans, jugs and chopping boards. At the end of his speech he had a queue of customers; and I had a chef's jacket, Mark had a hat which made him look about seven-foot tall, and we had a set of measuring jugs 'which every French woman has and knows it is the secret to good cooking', along with a miniature silver table sweeper. The wily salesman threw in a wooden butter pat (that's never going to be used) for good measure, shook our hands, plunged his nose into the bag of garlic, sighed deeply with happiness and turned to serve the rest of his customers.

At the end of the day, we watched the Bastille Day fireworks fly off the ramparts. In the main square, a band played jazz manouche music. In our ringside seats at a café on the square we listened to the classic sound of France in the warm air, guaranteed to make you feel relaxed as you sip a glass of wine.

After the month we'd had, it was good to feel like we were getting back to normal.

Half full, or half empty?

'I SUPPOSE IT will be raining when we come to yours,' said my friend Suzanne on the phone. She sounded distinctly underwhelmed. 'We might have a few showers,' I concurred.

When people talk of Pas-de-Calais and don't live here, the first thing they always say is, 'Doesn't it rain a lot?' When I visit the south of France and tell people where I live, I get looks of sympathy, followed by confusion. 'But why would you live in the north? It pours all the time!' they protest.

'Should I bring books and boardgames?' said Suzanne.

'Why would you do that?' I asked, nonplussed.

'Well, something to do when it rains? Bobby doesn't like to be bored.' Bobby is her husband. I knew Suzanne from the days when we had worked in a bank together and I hadn't seen her for at least five years, during which time she'd met and married Bobby, a senior equity trader.

We regularly emailed each other and she'd asked if they could stay for a few days en route to their rented holiday villa near Nice.

'For one, it doesn't rain that much,' I assured her, 'and even if it does, there's loads to do. For starters there are more museums in this region than any other, apart from Île de France of course, which has Paris.' She told me that they would dress appropriately. 'I've read your book,' she said. 'We know what to expect.'

We were still reeling from the damage the storm had done to the house. The rain that had flooded in through the roof had dried out, but the ceilings in several rooms needed to be repaired where the wet plaster had cracked and split, and some rooms needed repainting where the water had run down the walls. The broken loft windows, covered in protective plastic, would have to be ripped out and replaced. The woodshed roof was destroyed and, as it wasn't covered by insurance, would have to be our next job so we could make sure we had dry wood for the winter. The greenhouse was now just a metal frame and a pile of glass but, as it wasn't a priority, it would have to wait until next year. We knew by this stage that our plans to finish the house by the end of the year were going to fail. Visitor distraction seemed like a good idea.

Suzanne and Bobby arrived in Calais in time for lunch so I'd booked them a table at the fabulous restaurant Le

Channel, on Boulevard de la Résistance along the seafront. This part of Calais has a bit of a fishing village vibe with small boats bobbing in the little harbour, but you can still see the huge ferries floating majestically by, shuttling millions of passengers each year between Calais and Dover. The restaurant is run by the family Crespo. Madame is the consummate meeter and greeter, and one of her sons is a chef, while the other is maître d'. It's been a favourite with locals and savvy Brits for over forty years, and we know regular visitors who time their trips so that they can stop for lunch or dinner there. The oysters and locally caught fresh fish dishes are legendary, while gastronomes swoon over the sweet cart, everything made by the onsite pâtisserie chef. The cheese cloche has been known to make some sigh out loud with happiness.

After shopping at the big wine stores and outlet centre, then taking the scenic route along the Opal Coast as I'd recommended, our friends arrived at our house late in the afternoon. Bobby beeped the hooter on his Porsche convertible (lid up against the rain he was convinced would fall) to let us know they had arrived.

His first words were about the grey sky and the prospect of a wet barbecue, which we'd organized for that night in honour of their arrival, having also invited along some of our neighbours. Mark assured him the weather would be fine –

local weather expert Claudette had passed by earlier, telling us that we might expect a smattering of rain but that was it.

'We would have been here sooner,' said Suzanne, 'but we got held up just around the corner by a herd of cows crossing the road!'

'It's bloody ridiculous. I got shit all over my tyres,' said Bobby.

'Your septic tank's all right now, isn't it?' Suzanne said to me, laughing.

'What septic tank?' said Bobby, looking alarmed.

'You know, babe, I told you Janine's got a septic tank and it blew up! It's what all the waste goes into cos they don't have mains drains here. What was inside spread all over the garden and everyone here calls her Madame Merde!'

'What? Over this garden, where we're having the barbecue?' Bobby looked horrified when he spotted the table and chairs laid out on the terrace.

'It was years ago,' I told him. 'A lot of rain has fallen since then, and what came out of the tank has long gone. And anyway, I think I'm known as the Pig Lady now as some people seem to believe I keep pigs in the house.'

'You don't, do you?' said Bobby, looking nervously over my shoulder at the house.

'No, of course not!' I said, laughing. 'It was all a misunderstanding with the Bread Man when I was telling him I work in the pigsty.' I hastily explained about the pigsty now being a beautiful and clean office. 'Mark built me my dream writing room with shelves for my thousands of books, and we have desks where we sit opposite each other and work …'

Bobby rolled his eyes at that. 'Could you imagine us working opposite each other all day, babe?' he said to Suzanne, who shook her head as we walked down the long garden path with their luggage. I thought to myself how charmingly uncoiffed the garden looked. Under a cloudy sky, the emerald-coloured lawn was dotted with trees festooned with flowers and vibrant green leaves. Pink and white roses and deep purple clematis clambered over the hawthorn hedges. Pears, apples and quinces were ripening on trees dotted around the garden and the scent of honeysuckle perfumed the air.

The chickens had run to the bottom of the garden and returned to the pens when they heard the car's hooter. Even Ken, whose behaviour was becoming worse by the day, had retreated. (He had now taken to standing as close as he could to me at every given opportunity and doing a bizarre little jig. Jean-Claude had told me this meant that Ken saw me as his woman.)

Over a glass of wine, Suzanne told us she'd loved Le Channel and the drive to our house along the coastal road, the D940, which wends its wiggly way through tiny fishing villages. We chatted about the old days when we worked together, the long hours and the bitchy bosses, and from what Suzanne said, it didn't sound as if much had changed. Bobby talked about his work, which he loved, and the smart restaurants he took his clients to and how much money he earned. Everything seemed to be going well until he wandered down to the bird pens in his smart loafers and trod in chicken poo.

'Darling,' said Suzanne, 'I told you we were staying on a farm and to wear your old shoes.'

'These are my old shoes, babe,' he said angrily. 'Shit.'

'You'll be fine if you don't go in the pens and keep to the paths,' I told him as he pushed his hands impatiently through his immaculately styled hair and stomped into the house to change into another, equally smart pair of shoes.

He returned with his mobile phone, having logged into our wifi, which isn't good even in the house. The signal barely reaches the garden so he fiddled with his phone constantly, trying to read his emails, which, when they arrived, prompted a loud and irritating bing-bong-bing-bong-pluck notification alert. I've never been so pleased to have intermittent internet.

When our French friends arrived for the barbecue, there were kisses and handshakes all round. We'd invited the Wood

Club, but half of them were away on holiday, so it was just Petit Frère and Claude Sr, Jean-Claude and Bernadette, plus Constance and Guillaume, and the Parisians, who we now knew as Hubert and Valerie (though she'd told us to call her Vava, as her friends did). We'd been to their house for drinks a couple of nights before as they were spending the whole of August in the village. Vava is a headmistress at a school in Paris and speaks perfect English. They knew of the area through Hubert's former colleague who they called Le Flic (French slang for police detective). He had retired to Le Touquet, but struggled to get to grips with the strong accent and dialect of the locals. I lent them my Ch'ti dictionary (yes, there really is such a thing). Drinks had become dinner and we'd talked for hours.

The barbecue was the first time Jean-Claude had a chance to talk to the Parisians and I could see he was charmed. They weren't at all the aloof and snooty city slickers everyone had been expecting, and when Vava whipped the Ch'ti dictionary out of her bag to look something up as she was chatting to him, the rest of the French guests fell about laughing, as Jean-Claude has the strongest accent of them all.

The barbecue smoked pleasantly, the juicy piquant green olives I'd bought in Le Touquet were praised, and Mark's pasta salad got a round of applause. Vava talked in English to

French are admittedly as much in love with their mobile phones as the rest of the world, it's rare to see people using them while they are eating out with friends or family.

Around eleven o'clock, Suzanne said she was ready for bed. They had been on the go since the early hours of the morning and it had been a long and tiring week. We stayed up a while chatting to our French friends – nobody said a word about Bobby – and they left after helping us clear away the dishes. 'Do you think we've become French?' said Mark, as we lay in bed, talking about the day. I'd been thinking the same thing. Life in London was a world I'd been away from long enough to look back on with fondness, mostly because I was younger then, but I was definitely glad I wasn't a part of it any longer. I certainly didn't miss the early starts and late nights with takeaway meals as it was always too late to cook, working weekends in the office and never having enough time to see Mark or my family. But it was about more than that. We'd learned to savour a good glass of wine, to take time over a meal and appreciate the hard work of the person who'd made it, whether that was a humble cook or a great chef. We'd gradually shrugged off the cloak of detachment that all city dwellers develop as a form of protection to preserve some personal space in a crowded environment. We were friendly to our neighbours and courteous to strangers.

When we meet someone new, we instinctively say *bonjour* instead of trying to edge away and avoid eye contact as we did in London. When I go to London these days, I speak to people in shops. When I take the bus, I say hello to the drivers and the people who work at railway stations. It's become instinctive and I've found it's contagious. Far more people talk to me than they used to, though obviously there are some that just look at me silently with furrowed brows.

In the morning, we walked the dogs early as usual and sat in the garden with a cup of tea under an umbrella as a light drizzle fell. Suzanne came out without Bobby. He was packing, she said. She was very apologetic, but said that they had decided to leave earlier than planned, after breakfast. With just three weeks off work, they really needed some sunshine and had decided to get going to the south. 'Totally get that,' said Mark, a bit too quickly.

We waved them *au revoir* as the Porsche roared down our little hill, setting off all the neighbourhood dogs. The sun came out the next day and the rest of the month was glorious.

Like the Parisians, the whole of France seems to go on holiday in August, though generally, unlike Hubert and Vava, the French too head south. Many shops close, and restaurateurs too take weeks off at a time during the busiest season of the year. Half of me rather likes that family and 'me' time means more to them than making money. The other half of me thinks they must be totally bonkers.

The farmers, of course, never get a holiday in August. They work flat out looking after animals and crops, assessing the perfect time for harvesting and sometimes working all through the night if wet weather looms and threatens to ruin a field full of ripe hay. Some tractors are big and modern like Thierry's – he sinks all of his money into modern equipment because he and Mathilde do most of the work between them and have a lot of land to cover. Some families often use the same old tractors they've had for decades.

Those that stay put in these parts spend sunny days on the beautiful sandy beaches of the Opal Coast, and it sometimes feels as if the roads are full of ancient drivers, pottering to the coast, with no interest in using signals of any sort, as if to say 'Whose business it is of anyone else's where I'm going?' We, too, would normally make the most of the stunning seaside towns on our doorstep in the summer months. But we had a roof to repair.

I try to avoid going into the woodshed because it's dark and spiders weave jumbo-sized webs across the walls and ceiling, but we needed to make the most of the good weather and get on with replacing the tiles. Mark climbed up onto the roof and threw the broken ones onto a pile, ready to reuse to make garden paths. He passed any whole tiles to me and I stacked them in a corner to reuse for the roof or to share with neighbours who might need them. The activity provoked spiders to run up the walls and across the floor and parachute down from the rickety old rafters. If you happened to have been passing by a French farmhouse in a tiny hamlet in the middle of nowhere in rural northern France one August day and heard shrieking from a shed, followed by the sight of a small woman hurtling up the garden flapping her arms – it might have been me.

We soon discovered that fixing the roof would involve more than just tiling. The ancient roof batons were rotten and the joists were just about clinging onto the rafters, which were also in state of decrepitude. We realized we would have to reinforce the whole lot before we laid the new tiles.

It took us the rest of the month to finish and Mark later informed me that he had gained the sympathy of every man in the village that summer. They had seen him render the walls of the house and the garden, paint the house, and afterwards put up trellises for the roses to grow up. He had hung the shutters, built steps to the front gate and the door, spread 5 tons of gravel on the 100-foot-long front path and erected a vertical herb garden in the courtyard.

When Mark went to walk the dogs, he bumped into Jean-Claude, who shook his hand saying, '*Le chef* [boss], she has you working today, *mon ami*?' and nodded to his own house where Bernadette can often be heard shrieking for her husband so she can tell him what needs to be done that day. 'The young man who built his own house' also came out to commiserate. He's known by that name to everyone in the village as we all watched in awe three years ago as he set about turning a simple wooden barn into a *manoir* for the love of his life. He worked day and night and, thankfully, his true love married him at the end of the build. Monsieur with the white horses and Petite Frère all nod, apparently with sympathy, at Mark's plight. Clearly I am now viewed as a house-proud, bossy madame in the village. Never mind that I get up at six in the morning to paint shutters, or that I put down my writing pen to help out with the rest of the jobs that need doing, from mixing concrete to plastering walls.

We finished the roof and, as a reward, treated ourselves to a meal at Friterie Francky, a café in the front garden of a house in the neighbouring tiny village of Manninghem-au-Mont. It's the equivalent of Cheers – the bar in the TV series where everyone knows your name. You can tell if it's open as orange lights flash on the gateposts.

As you go through the gate there's a terrace with tables and chairs, colourful umbrellas, lights in the trees and flowers everywhere. Eighties disco music fills the air.

Everyone in the terrace area says *bonjour*, shakes hands with you or kisses you on the cheek, so sometimes it can take a while before you can place your order. When we do make it into the café, Francky stops cooking and hops round from the kitchen to plant kisses on our cheeks (two in this area). His partner Arnaud comes around from the counter, more kisses, then we shake hands or exchange kisses with everyone inside. There are two dining areas inside and when you get to them, there are more *bonjours*, kisses and handshakes. Then the '*bon apps*' start (shortened from *bon appetit*). When it's time to leave we start again with the *au revoirs*, kisses and handshakes.

At the end of the month, our friend Paul popped by to make sure we were definitely going to be there in October for his wedding to Delphine. I was feeling particularly generous that morning, and Paul took full advantage of my good mood, spending an hour telling us where he met Delphine, which we already knew, and how much he loves her, which everyone knows as he makes no secret of it, kissing her often in public with real passion. If talking was an Olympic sport, Paul would be a gold medallist. He can speak for hours and hours on end. And does – if you don't know better and allow him to get going, it's very difficult to get him to stop, though Delphine often just tells him to be quiet. But he is also witty, generous-natured and kind, so, although he can go on a bit, we all forgive him for it.

In fact, being able to talk for hours on end is considered a very good thing in France. At school French kids learn to debate as a matter of course. A wildly popular French TV documentary in 2016 called *À voix haute* (Speak Up) pulled in the viewers with its marketing, which read: 'Speaking well is the key to social advancement and what is better than a beautiful and long speech? Nothing. Is not a beautiful and long speech to be heard, understood and acclaimed? It is an ancient art that has a name: eloquence …' The programme followed teenagers who took part in verbal contests to prove their oral worth by 'arguing, whispering, arguing more, laughing, haranguing and arguing again'. They even have a TV show in France called *Le Grand Oral*, which definitely isn't as exciting as it might sound to some. Twelve amateur speakers compete against each other to give the best speech before a jury – not the sort of talent show to which most of us are used. It's very earnest and there's not a lot of laughing. French audiences lap it up – the more passionate, dramatic and eloquent the speaker, the more the French seem utterly mesmerized. One of the speeches gained more than 10 million views on social media networks.

The adage that 'sometimes not speaking says more than all the words in the world' doesn't apply in France. I wondered what Paul's wedding speech would be like …

Fifty-two ducks and one Ducasse

HARVEST TIME IS also party time in the Seven Valleys and the mayor had organized a *Ducasse* at the town hall. It has absolutely nothing to do with the great French chef Alain Ducasse, but is an old Flemish word meaning festival.

When a *Ducasse* is held, the entire village is invited to join in. There's always dinner – nothing formal or stuffy, usually mussels or fried chicken and always frites and copious amounts of beer, wine or cider. It's followed by dancing and often goes on until the early hours of the morning. Although there are only 142 people in this village, socialites from miles around reserve tickets for what is claimed to be one of the biggest nights of the year in these parts.

Forty-eight hours before the big day, a marquee was put up in the car park of the town hall (formerly the village school). The DJ came the afternoon before the party to test the sound quality, and we could hear Gloria Gaynor assuring us she would survive and Kool and the Gang urging us to get down on it reverberating around the valleys, making the cows moo and the dogs howl.

Always held on a Saturday, the party kicked off at 7.30. A steady stream of people began to fill the tent and take their seats at long tables laid out in neat rows on either side, with an aisle down the middle. By using very thin benches, not unlike the church's pews, they managed to squeeze in a staggering 420 people. Not everyone sits – a few craggy-faced farmers always stand at the makeshift bar at the front, holding their Picon beers or a glass of robust ruby-red wine, surveying the room like ageing Mafia dons at a country wedding. Kids run around, getting under everyone's feet, pretending to be riding horses and sliding on their knees on the wooden floor. The old folk always sit on the front tables so they can leave before the dancing starts without climbing over other guests.

There was a lot of toing and froing as trays filled with glasses and bottles from the bar were precariously carried back to tables. Even Thierry the farmer and his wife Mathilde were there, enjoying a rare night off. It had been a difficult year for them with storm-damaged crops, so they really did deserve to let their hair down.

'Did you see Mathilde?' said my friend Annette. 'She's not wearing her green boiler suit!' This was big news – she hadn't been seen outside her green boiler suit in years. 'I missed her,' I said to Annette. 'What was she wearing?' I was hoping for something glitzy: sequins, high-heeled shoes, dangly earrings …

'Green top and green trousers,' grinned Annette.

The new mayor made a speech, of course. He talked about how we would all pull together to get the village back on track, and that work would be starting in earnest soon to cover roofs before winter. He welcomed friends from 'near and far' (though hardly anyone is from further than 10 km away), as well as the Parisians and the Anglais.

In order to avoid the usual pandemonium when it came to queueing up to get entrées from the buffet table at the back of the tent, this year, he informed us, we would all be called by table number. 'Table 1, come and get your entrée,' led to an eruption of wild cheers and clapping. The oldies lined up to go to the buffet, making their way down the centre aisle to claps and whistles. If they had been supermodels twirling about in the latest Louis Vuitton outfits, they wouldn't have got a better reception. As they returned with plates heaving with vegetable salad, diced beetroot, grated carrot, pâté and bread, more applause erupted.

'Table 2 come up and get your entrée,' was even more enthusiastically received. We clearly had a new contest between the tables, fuelled by copious amounts of alcohol, to see who could be the noisiest. Twenty tables, each seating twenty people – it took hours to get the entrées over with as people couldn't make up their minds whether to have the salad, the beetroot or the carrots, or both, and with or without pâté – bread, of course, was a given. Earlier on, the Bread Man had dropped off hundreds of baguettes – a special vanload just for this night.

Finally, by ten o'clock, the smell of the main meal wafted in through the tent door: heaps of French fries (which are actually Belgian) cooked in boiling vats in a mobile chip wagon in the car park, and chicken cooked over a massive oil-drum barbecue manned by Tomas. His face was red and sweaty as he toiled in the roasting heat, the flames of the barbecue whipped up by the wind whooshing through the valley, heralding the arrival of autumn and making the sides of the marquee quiver. This time, volunteers carried the main-course dishes to the tables, speeding things up a little. Swiftly clearing away, they followed with slivers of cheese and cornichons, those piquant pickles you only ever seen in France, and finally a selection of petit four cakes, eclairs and madeleines, tiny lemon meringue tarts and crunchy merveilles, a meringue balloon filled with cream.

By midnight, everyone had finally finished. Tomas and the frites-van staff came in for a well-deserved drink and a round of applause. The oldies made their escape, not keen on the loud music. The disco lights were switched on, and the new mayor pushed a button on the turntable to release the sounds of Right Said Fred's 'I'm Too Sexy'. The marquee was bathed in rainbow colours as the DJ burst through the entrance, resplendent in a pair of tight black plastic trousers and a white vest stretched tight across his ample body, sporting the words 'Superstar of the music machine' and cut low, revealing an impressive mass of chest hair. He made his way to the back of the tent accompanied by whoops and cheers, turned on the microphone and shouted '*Allez, allez, allez.*' He put on the slower number 'Joue Pas de Rock 'n' Roll pour Moi' by Johnny Hallyday, which felt a bit anticlimactic, but electrified the partygoers nonetheless. There was a stampede to the dancefloor and hours of line dancing and every other kind of dancing ensued.

Jean-François, almost unrecognizable out of his blue overalls, was wearing a smart shirt and jogging pants. He made us all jump when he stamped the wooden floor with lusty abandon in a Flamenco-style display – which he then repeated for every single tune. Seventy-year-old Marie-Thérèse, who uses a walking stick, swayed along to the Eurythmics. People jived and jumped, twisted and dipped, spun and shook their tail feathers with gusto and total *joie de vivre* until the sun peeped up over the hills. The next week, many of the partygoers would do it all again at another harvest party in another village.

It was also the time for *la rentrée*, a term used to describe the particularly French phenomenon that signals that summer is over. It is the cue for everyone to return to work, school and normality after the long summer holidays. Despite this, there's really nothing sad about this season – quite the opposite. There's a feeling of enthusiasm and joy in the air. And best of all, the restaurants throw open their shutters to welcome back customers and the shops are all open, too.

Over the next few weeks, keen gardeners would be harvesting as much as they could, and keen cooks would be making jam, chutneys and sauces, and freezing summer fruits and vegetables. Potatoes would be dug up and hoarded in cellars, carrots stored in boxes of sand. Soon pumpkins would be ready for harvesting and there is always a contest to see who has grown the biggest in the village. One year, a green-fingered monsieur managed to grow one so large no one could lift it and it had to be rolled into a tractor bucket to be taken out of the garden. If four wheels had been put on it, I think I could have driven it into town.

Gardeners and cooks are not the only ones preparing for winter. Wild pigs, deer and birds of all kinds start some serious foraging, and my adopted hedgehogs (by now there were at least eight of them regularly feeding at the back door) started to eat more, preparing for hibernation. The ducks, geese and chickens enjoy autumn perhaps more than any other season as they are the beneficiaries of the glut of apples we have every year. The dogs love to run in the cooler weather, and when the farmers cut the fields of sweetcorn (maize) they race down the neat lines, searching for grouse and pheasant, which they never catch.

La rentrée also brought a call from the roofing company, who were due to repair our house in November. A slot had come up unexpectedly and they would start the next week. We were delighted. Although we had become accustomed to the sight of the roof covered in tarpaulins, flapping about in the wind, we were thrilled that we would be watertight before the weather changed.

I was up way before the sun rose on the day the roofers were due. I couldn't sleep for excitement and headed to the pigsty with a cup of tea to write in peace and quiet. At five o'clock in the morning, the quarter moon didn't give much light but the stars twinkled like diamonds in a black velvet bag. An owl hooted in Claudette's barn, irritated that I'd put a light on to find my way across the courtyard. Another owl replied, no doubt agreeing that I was inconsiderate. Pheasants made weird croaking noises in the hedges and flapped their wings nervously. Moths flew in and out of the beams of light.

Brad Pitt and George Clooney became very excited when they saw me. Any form of light means sunup for them, even if it's just a torch. Their hollering set off Kendo Nagasaki and Gregory Peck, the older cockerels. Then the geese started running around squealing like they had seen a ghost. Two cats stuck their heads out of the woodshed door to see what the fuss was all about. I almost trod on a hedgehog that had fallen asleep in one of the cat-food bowls and let out a screech, though by this time you could hardly say it shattered the tranquillity of the countryside. The only thing missing by now was a marching mariachi band.

Four burly builders turned up promptly at eight o'clock with a lorryload of scaffolding. Not stopping for coffee, they immediately began unloading and completed the job by the end of the day. The next day, five builders arrived together with a lorryload of tiles, which were craned into the front garden, and an enormous skip for the broken tiles. They scampered about on the roof of the main house all day long, forming a human chain to remove all the tiles, salvaging any that weren't broken and neatly stacking them for us to reuse. The broken windows were removed before they laid a roofing membrane to make sure the house was protected against rain.

On day three, two tilers turned up – wiry men who looked like brothers, with their dark hair, dark eyes and deep tans. This was our first experience of working with French artisans as we had handled the entire renovation by ourselves until now. They were incredibly polite and hard-working and, contrary to the popular stereotype, they turned up on time every day. They took plenty of breaks, sipping thick, sugary, milk-less coffee from tiny cups, and every day asked to plug a lead into our electricity so that they could use their microwave oven in the back of their van. We could see them through our side door, sitting at a table they had brought with them, enjoying a three-course lunch and glass of red wine. The aroma of stews and strong cheese wafted around our garden, attracting the attention of passers-by, as well as the local dogs and cats.

The weather stayed mostly dry and they made good progress roaming around on the roof. Music from their portable radio blasted out over the sound of tiles being hammered into place. Surprisingly, they were very partial to an English singalong. I wasn't sure if it was for our benefit but as I sat working in the pigsty I could hear them warbling an out-of-tune version of 'You Are the Sunshine of My Life', whistling when they didn't know the words, and a spirited rendition of 'Rrrrra-rrrrra Rrrrrasputeen, lover of the Rrrrrussian Queen'.

Not everyone was pleased at the activity, especially Frank Bruno, our rescue dog. He likes things to be quiet and calm, and all that banging about on the roof made him very tetchy. Churchill, the friendly German pinscher, loves attention. He had grown up in a glass cage in a pet shop before we took him home (as no one else wanted him and he would have been put down), so he was used to lots of people being around. He will happily follow anyone and everyone, and just wants more and more friends. Ella Fitzgerald is the love of Frank Bruno's life. She grew up in the cage with Churchill and he would howl all night long for her, only stopping when we went back to the shop to get her, too. She is scared of her own shadow, and watched the roofers toing and froing with doleful eyes from within her little house in the garden. The geese, too, were indignant, honking at the strangers from afar (seriously, nothing ever happens in this village), but the chickens and ducks wouldn't give a stuff if Father Christmas was up on the roof as long as they were fed.

The roofing repairs went on for a fortnight, exactly as had been estimated. I have to say that I didn't like the new roof. It looked way too spick and span compared to the worn tiles we had before, but Mark assured me that a few seasons and plenty of rain would see it looking less shiny, and it would soon be dotted with the moss with which we were familiar. The important thing was that we were ready for winter. And the roofers predicted the roof would long outlive me and would stand up to large hailstones in the unlikely event that it ever happened again. Their boss came around to sign off the forms and brought a bottle of champagne. He was a very happy man – he had enough work from the village to last him many months to come. The storm clouds had a silver lining for some.

The village was buzzing to the sound of hammers banging that autumn, with saws whizzing and the coming and going of delivery vans and lorries. Under blue skies and a warm autumnal sun, the tarpaulins were coming off, new tiles were going up, and our neighbours were taking this as an opportunity to tidy up gardens, repair fences and paint shutters. It wasn't a speedy process, though. With a finite number of builders to go round, some people were still waiting for their repairs to start. And there was Jean-Claude, who only had a few broken tiles on his relatively new roof, but was holding out for a complete replacement, driving Bernadette mad with his stubbornness but eventually wearing the insurers down.

With one big job done, it was time to deal with our duck problem. Even though I had become vigilant about collecting eggs, the final toll of hatchlings was high and that year became known as the 'summer of fifty-two ducklings'.

Jean-Claude told us that if you have more than fifty birds you must register as a farm, and we were now over the limit despite having rehoused several over the summer.

In the meantime, the daily feeding routine had become nothing less than a ruckus. Ducks and chickens wandered about seemingly at will, flying over the fences of the pens where I wished they would stay, or finding holes to squeeze through, and any vegetables that hadn't been destroyed by the storm were devoured. Every morning my first job was to feed and clean the birds. As I groggily pulled on rubber boots in the kitchen, the birds would spot me and a flock of them would come winging across the garden to the back door, quacking and clucking. They pecked my boots, hung off my sleeves, climbed into the food bins and clung to the buckets of food while I was on my way to the pens.

I set to finding new homes for as many ducks as possible, and by the end of the month we'd shunted them all over the locality to kind-hearted families who wanted pets (and assured me they wouldn't eat them). We also gave some to Annette, who has a huge garden with a pond and adores ducks – she took half of them in one go. The result was that I was left with nine boys and two girls, including Belle and her daughter Bella, with whom I couldn't bear to part. To be sure we didn't repeat our rookie mistakes, the girls were put in a separate pen from the boys this time.

But the bird fun wasn't over. We still had to deal with crazy Ken. I felt a bit like Inspector Clouseau in the garden, waiting for Cato to attack. He was starting to really worry me as he was even worse with strangers. Barbie, the other abandoned chicken, had grown into a beauty and had the sweetest nature, and was happy to be stroked. Ken, on the other hand, was not remotely grateful for the special treatment he had been given. He charged at anyone who came into the garden. He didn't get on with the other birds either and had caused mayhem in the pens. He tried it on with all the girls, but they just brushed him off and fixed their beady eyes on him. Despite his aggressive behaviour with humans, he was more of a coward with Kendo Nagasaki and Roger Moore, the pen leaders, and would swiftly escape back into the garden whenever he encountered them.

When our British friend Guy popped in on his way home from a holiday in the south, we sat in the kitchen to have a natter and enjoy the view of the garden, which was lush and verdant in the warm sun of an Indian summer. Out of the corner of my eye, I spotted Ken under the gazebo, with Barbie following him about as usual. 'He seems pretty tame,' said Guy. 'I thought you called him Psycho Ken.'

'He hasn't seen you yet,' I said. And, right on cue, Ken looked up. 'Now he's seen you.'

Ken pulled himself up as tall as he could, ruffled up his neck feathers and thrust his chest out, looking indignant that an intruder had come into his territory.

'He's going to run down the garden and throw himself at the door, stare at you and then sing a song,' I warned Guy. He looked at me sceptically. But sure enough, Ken began to take off down the garden towards us at a ferocious pace, threw himself at the door, stared hard at Guy and burst into a very loud crow with a sigh at the end. I always thought he sounded a bit like Minnie Riperton singing 'Lovin'You' during these episodes. Guy and I both laughed, which seemed to wind up Ken even more. He crowed, jumped up and down and flapped his wings, knocking things over on the terrace outside the back door.

Meanwhile Barbie ran around the terrace and the geese started honking wildly. George Clooney, the biggest cockerel in the garden, jumped up into a tree and was swinging wildly like a trapeze artist. Rambo the duck decided to climb the fence to sit and watch the fun, which made all the other ducks quack and it sounded just like they were laughing. I wondered if, as well as Miss Poule and Mr Coq beauty contests, there might also be scope for a Coq and Poule talent competition.

Ken didn't like the Bread Man either. Whenever he heard the van arrive he would run to the gate and I would

but I couldn't think of a single instance without a silent 'h'. Later, I asked my French-teacher friend Delphine why this might be. French people make the 'h' sound when they laugh, so why not when they talk? Apparently it's because Frenchies think that their language is the most beautiful in the world and flows perfectly – and fitting in a hard 'h' would make it *'orrible*. Delphine also told me they even have a sort of language police in France, guardians dedicated to protecting the French language – mostly from foreign word invasion! The Académie Française was created in 1635 by Cardinal Richelieu in an attempt to make the French language 'pure and comprehensible to all'. Ever since then, except for ten years when the French Revolution put them out of business, their forty members, known as 'the immortals', have looked after French words – both new and old. They are based in a beautiful building in Paris, opposite the Louvre, and have an official uniform, a long black coat with gold embroidery rumoured to cost £40,000, and that doesn't include the sword they have to carry for official engagements – presumably to cut through the claptrap. It's a very elitist group made up of writers, historians and even politicians. If an English word creeps into popular usage, the Académie Française will come up with an alternative and urge everyone in France to use it. 'Parking' for instance, which is what Frenchies say when referring to a parking space for a car, should, according to the Académie Française dictionary, be '*Aire de stationnement*'. But it's a bit of a mouthful, isn't it? So everyone just says 'le parking'.

Bread Man told me he'd read in that day's newspaper that forecasters were predicting 'the coldest winter on record'.

'They say that every year,' I said.

'One of these year's they'll be right,' he replied.

Last winter's prediction for the snowy apocalypse couldn't have been more wrong. It was positively balmy in the north of France. Not like our first winter in this old house when the temperatures plummeted to -20°C. The fire wasn't working properly and at night, huddled around an oil heater, wrapped up in duvets, we watched our breath make frost patterns in the cold air inside the house.

Later that afternoon, Jean-Claude was passing as we returned home from a visit to the Wood Man to order more wood for the winter, adding to our supplies from the Wood Club. His squeaky wheelbarrow was filled with pumpkins – big orange ones, ornate green ones and long creamy-coloured ones. His garden is full of them at this time of the year and he's extremely proud to hold the title for 'Biggest Pumpkin of the Valleys'.

'Got to get these into storage,' he told us as we were unpacking the wood from the car. 'It's going to be the coldest winter on record.'

To bise or not to bise ...

BACK HOME, A delicate breeze swished through the valleys and spun the golden leaves, which fell from trees starting to prepare themselves for colder weather. Fluffy clouds floated across a clear blue sky, and the light had a mellow lustre, the sort you only get on a sunny day in autumn in the north of France. The scent of fermenting apples hung in the air as, all around the village, spirited cider-making sessions were taking place in barns and cellars. Winter was on the doorstep. When Belle, one of the two female ducks we had left, hatched two eggs, I was flabbergasted, and not just because it was the wrong time of the year. The two girls had been separated from the boys, and we had thought that there had been no more fraternizing. We could only assume that they had managed, ninja-like, to scale the fences in order to have their secret moment of passion before sneaking back into their respective pens. The Juliets and Romeos of the poultry world.

When Jean-Claude stopped by for a chat and a glass of wine, I asked him how he thought the affair of the immaculately conceived ducklings could have happened, but he didn't seem surprised. 'Where there's a will there's a way,' he told me. I also quizzed him about what to do with Psycho Ken, who was worrying me more and more. The sweet abandoned chick we'd found in the woods in the spring had long since gone, and it seemed his feathery body had been taken over by a demon.

I had tried everything I could to get him to behave. I'd even spoken to a specialist chicken vet who advised me to try to soothe him, talk to him and pick him up to get him used to contact. But this just seemed to enrage Ken further and he pecked at my face. He was now chasing Mark, too, as well as the cats and dogs and anyone who came into the garden. I tried keeping him in a pen with high fences, but he was like a winged Houdini, and nothing seemed to be able to contain him. I was worried that if we had kids in the garden, he could cause a serious injury.

'Have you ever had a bird gone bad?' I asked Jean-Claude.

'Many times,' he replied. 'Sometimes male birds are just naturally aggressive and there's not much you can do about it. They have to be let go.' I gulped. I knew what he meant by letting go.

I took Jean-Claude to the pen where I was keeping Ken, but he'd escaped again, and he began stalking us around the garden like the cunning velociraptor in *Jurassic Park*. He seemed utterly incensed that there was a trespasser in his territory and flew at Jean-Claude feet first. Jean-Claude might be on the wrong side of sixty, but he's a wily Frenchman. He moved swiftly to one side and deftly caught the screeching Ken, tipping him upside down to calm him.

'No, no,' he said gravely, 'this one you cannot keep. He'll have your eyes out.'

My lips quivered. I couldn't bear the thought of Ken being put down. For all his faults, he had the most amazing cock-a-doodle-doo, a high-pitched screech and always a low hum at the end, like a sigh. 'He's very beautiful, though,' said Jean-Claude, and then left with the bird before I could change my mind. I felt very bad about Ken for a while, but it was nice not to have to wear protective clothes to peg out the washing.

Three weeks later I heard a familiar sound, a high-pitched cock-a-doodle-doo … le sigh. It came from Jean-Claude's garden. I got a chair and climbed up to look over the high hedge. There was Ken, in a large maximum-security pen with no chance of parole, but his good looks had won him a reprieve and a couple of female companions.

Over the last few years, Halloween, which used to be largely ignored, especially here in the rural far north, has become much more popular. Go back five years and you'd hardly know it existed apart from in the boulangeries and chocolate shops, but now you'll find a few local shops decked out with festive spider webs, cardboard witches on brooms and singing pumpkins – the influence of US TV shows and Disney, I suspect. I don't mind any of it apart from the cobwebs.

The warm, wet autumn weather of the north is good for spiders. I'm not a fan of them. It was my dad's fault. He would run a mile if he saw one, screaming for my mum to come and deal with it. He was a master bridge player and once, overnighting in a posh hotel in Edinburgh in Scotland where he was to play a bridge tournament the next day, he was getting ready for bed when he spotted a small spider. He fled the room in his underpants. Security were called, and they searched the room, but the spider was nowhere to be seen. My dad swears he stayed awake all night with the light on, scanning the room, fully dressed by now, ready to flee again. He still won his bridge match, though.

I too am terrified of spiders even though I know it is ridiculous. We don't, as far as I know, get poisonous spiders in the north of France but *mon Dieu*, that October they were enormous. I'd never seen them that big before. Mark is not afraid at all: he picks them up and doesn't care if they run up his arms before taking them out to safety in the garden. I took to eyeballing a room before I entered. Some of the spiders were almost as big as the palm of my hand (admittedly I do have small hands) so you can't really miss them. Claudette told me to put piles of chestnuts around the house – the spiders crawled over them. I bought one of those machines that you plug in and is supposed to make them run away – within a week it was covered in webs.

Here in my little village we're not quite at the trick-or-treat stage but it can only be a matter of time before the kids brave the cold and the muddy paths to knock on doors. Quite what Claudette will make of it, I don't know. I'm pretty sure she has no idea that Halloween is widely celebrated as a festive occasion around the world. Although she watches her ancient TV, it's only to listen to the news or programmes that feature the British royal family, whom she adores. Halloween to her is the night before *La Toussaint*, All Saints Day, a time to remember loved ones no longer with us.

If you walk up the hill that leads past the home of Jean-Claude and Bernadette, you might well think this is a village of the possessed since the fields at the top are peppered with gloomy-faced villagers waving mobile phones around. It's not some weird custom – it's due to our lack of mobile phone signal, which makes people very tetchy. You can hardly bank, buy or do anything online these days without getting a text message with a code that is essential to complete the deal. In the middle-of-nowhere Seven Valleys, this is a big problem. In our house, we draw straws for which of us must wander the fields, like the ghost of Mary Malone, until we hit a hotspot and can retrieve the coveted code to convey to the other one, sitting resignedly by the landline, waiting for numbers to type into the PC confirming, yes we did send a bank transfer/amend a standing order/purchase something. We never thought when we bought this house in 2004 that all these years later we would still be waiting for a mobile phone signal or fast internet.

The new mayor is valiant in his efforts to improve things. It's not an easy job. He updates us regularly on progress and puts copies of letters from those he petitions into our post box: 'We will review your request in about six weeks' time ... or maybe early next year ... We hope to make a decision sometime next year, or maybe the year after.'

The Bread Man wanted to know if we did anything special for Halloween. Not really, I told him, and wished him 'Happy Halloween.'

'Appy Alloween?' he queried.

'*Non*, *h*appy *H*alloween.' We were back on the 'h' issue again. I tried one more time, putting everything I had into a long, drawn-out hhhhhhh.

'Hhhhhhhhhe,' he went, 'hhhhhhhhhhhhhh.'

He was red-faced and hunched over with effort. The sound coming from deep within his body sounded, at best, as if he was in the grip of major respiratory problems and, at worst, highly inappropriate. Churchill the dog certainly relished the spectacle of Bread Man heavy breathing all over my baguette. He already liked him. Now he was positively in love.

The day of Paul and Delphine's wedding dawned with a beautiful pale pink sunrise. The official ceremony took place in the early afternoon in a town hall near Béthune where Delphine's family live. There's no shimmying up a rollercoaster, teetering on top of a tower or barefoot nuptials on a beach in France. And you can't even get married in a church. Here, every *mariage,* the French word that covers both wedding and marriage, has to go through a civil ceremony conducted by the mayor or their assistant in the local town hall. You can have a religious ceremony, too, but it doesn't count as an official *mariage*.

Going to a wedding is probably one of the few occasions when turning up on time is de rigueur, instead of plain rude and causing your hosts to suspect that you're possibly not fit for polite company. We arrived at the municipal town hall with ample time, we thought, at least thirty minutes early, but we hadn't considered that we would be meeting a lot of new people. Delphine and Paul, originally from the Gers department in the heartland of Gascony, invited forty close friends and family to join them and, as we knew only a few of them and there were a lot of introductions to be made and kisses to be given and received, we found ourselves sprinting round the guests.

To *bise* or not to *bise*? Even in France nobody actually knows how many times is correct to *faire la bise*, to kiss. There's even a website called combiendebises.com (How Many Kisses), which aims to help by allowing people to log how many kisses are appropriate in their region. Apparently, it's only one kiss in Finistère in Brittany, while those in some regions claim three, four or even a lip-smacking five kisses are required. And which side first, the left or the right? That differs too according to where you're from. It's best just to watch and see how the person opposite acts, and if in doubt go with two kisses, right cheek to right cheek first, as that is most common.

Everyone at the wedding was smartly dressed, but no tuxedos. 'They're only for meeting the president or going to a ball,' according to Jean-Claude, whom Bernadette had squashed into a suit for the occasion.

We crammed into the town hall and watched as Delphine and Paul tied the knot in a room with an open door, as is tradition, in case someone wished to burst in, object and shout 'It should have been me.' Since Paul's former squeeze, Sylvie, now lived in Béthune with her new beau, a baker, I did wonder if it might happen. But no, all went smoothly, and thirty minutes later the happy couple received their *Livret de famille*, a booklet that records main events within the family such as marriage, birth, death and divorce.

Leaving the building, they were subjected to a deluge of confetti, flower petals and rice before a group photo took place. We were all required to yell '*oustiti*', the equivalent of saying cheese, which forces you into a smile position (it's actually the French word for a marmoset). Some people think the French say '*fromage*', but I'm afraid it's not true.

Paul and Delphine left first in their car, white roses tied to the wing mirrors, to a hotel in the nearby town of Gosnay, and we soon followed to join the evening celebrations. Everyone beeped their horns constantly for the entire journey. If you've ever been in France on a Saturday afternoon, you'll probably have experienced this outpouring of hooter happiness. It's almighty racket is apparently is a hangover from the Middle Ages when people had a habit of getting married in secret, prompting the authorities to declare that weddings should be celebrated with as much noise as possible.

After we drove, still beeping, through the big wrought-iron gates of the hotel, we all parked in neat lines in front of the former chateau, noticing that every one of its grand windows was dripping with flowers. We dropped off luggage in a room that was decorated with richly patterned wallpaper in muted colours, plush, soft carpet and antique furnishings. The latticed windows of the hotel overlooked beehives. It was genteel, chic and charming but not remotely stuffy. The picturesque gardens were awash with early-evening autumn sunlight, and the sound of laughter and gentle conversation filtered through the wonderful ancient windows and doors. Candles flickered as the light started to fall, and immaculately dressed servers flitted in and out with champagne bottles and wooden boxes of succulent oysters.

Delphine's friends teased her that she was no longer a *Catherinette* and just in the nick of time, too, as St Catherine's Day, 25 November, was just around the corner. In France (feminists look away because you're not going to like this), unwed women used to be given bright yellow or green hats to wear on St Catherine's Day. They would put on their best clothes to match their hat and attend organized balls and parties in the hope of attracting a potential husband. Wearing hats isn't common practice any more, but shops do stock St Catherine cards to give to friends who have not yet found the partner of their dreams, and some people still wish their unmarried lady friends Happy St Catherine's Day.

Paul, who was looking very dapper (Delphine had expressly forbidden him to dress in any of his usual seventies gear), started his speech. We braced ourselves for a long night when he led us into an adjacent room in the hotel and fired up a PowerPoint presentation featuring mushrooms: Delphine picking mushrooms in the woods; Paul holding mushrooms up to his nose; mushrooms arranged in the shape of a heart on a table. All of the photos were captioned with romantic words by highly esteemed French people: '*Entre deux cœurs qui s'aiment, nul besoin de paroles*' ('Two hearts in love need no words') from a poem by Marceline Desbordes-Valmore; '*L'amour est l'emblème de l'éternité, il confond toute la notion de temps, efface toute la mémoire d'un commencement, toute la crainte d'une extrémité*' ('Love is the emblem of eternity; it confounds all notion of time, erases all memory of a beginning, all fear of an end') by nineteenth-century writer Madame de Staël. Paul read the words out solemnly, turning to gaze at a blushing Delphine, who looked as pleased as punch.

Dinner wasn't until a stomach-rumbling nine o'clock, but it was certainly worth the wait. The north met the south on the tables that night and it was a marriage made in heaven. Paul had informed us that the wedding date had been chosen specifically as it coincided with the optimal time for mushroom picking, so it came as no surprise that there were mushrooms of all shapes and sizes in the dishes. There was pork stuffed with chilli peppers and *saucisse chorizo*, vegetables from the hotel garden sprinkled with crystallized amaretto and quinoa tabbouleh with spices. Golden girolles sautéed in butter, mushrooms in cream and cognac, and warm chanterelles served with blackberries and Cantal cheese, a cousin of cheddar and a firm favourite in France for at least a thousand years.

There were lashings of ice-cold beer made locally, Gascon wines and finally a snifter of Armagnac from the Gers, which was mellow and heart-warming. The grand finale saw the lights dimmed, indoor fireworks lit and unexpectedly, the *Rocky* theme song. Then in came a *croquembouche*, a soaring column of bite-sized profiteroles, stuffed with cream, held together by crispy caramel and elaborately decorated with spun sugar and icing flowers. It was carried with utmost care by a waiter whose face was completely hidden by the towering dessert.

You would think by now we'd have all eaten ourselves to a standstill, but no, the night was young and dancing had to be done to an abundance of some of the worst music ever heard, personally chosen by Paul. When the obligatory 'Le Madison' was played, a tune that's been a crowd-pleaser consistently since the late 1950s, even Jean-Claude made his way to the dancefloor, becoming increasingly red as he hopped about to the beat.

In the morning, hungover but cheerful, we said goodbye to the happy couple who were off on their *lune de miel*, kissed all of our friends, new and old, and headed home to a rapturous welcome from cats and dogs, chickens, ducks and geese who, as much as they love babysitter Annette, seem to genuinely prefer me to clear up after them.

When I had asked the waiter in the hotel about the mushrooms that had been served at the wedding feast, he found out from the chef that they had come from a shop in Saint-Omer, a quintessential market town with one foot in the past, just half an hour's drive from Calais. They were honestly the best I'd ever had, and I knew I was going to have to seek them out. When it comes to markets, we're spoiled for choice. There are so many street markets to choose from within easy distance that I could go to a different one every day for a month and still have plenty left over. But the memory of the mushrooms remained, so the next Saturday we headed to Saint-Omer's morning market.

Wandering through the cobbled Grand Place (Place du Maréchal Foch) dominated by the neoclassical town hall, we were surrounded by the tantalizing smells that came from the street-food stalls, of tartiflette and couscous, and spit-roasted chicken turning over potatoes cooked in the juice that trickled down. I wandered over to a stall to buy some apples, and was impressed when the young lad serving asked me when I was planning to eat the apples and then proceeded to pick out the ones that would be best for me.

We bought a baguette straight from the oven at the boulangerie of Guy Delalleau, who sells the most divine cakes and breads. As we roamed the stalls I nibbled the end of it. Generally speaking, eating food in the street in France is considered a faux pas, but baguettes are the exception. No one has ever been known to have the willpower to resist the sweet aroma of a just-baked baguette.

Happiness is homemade

THIS TIME OF the year French churchyards, normally dour places, are transformed into a riot of colour. The first of November is All Saints Day and friends and family of the dearly departed take pots of vibrant chrysanthemums to place on graves. I always put flowers on the tomb of a young First World War British soldier from London, killed nearby and the only Commonwealth soldier buried in our local church. We've never seen any flowers on his grave and think it is likely that he has no one to remember him, so we do.

Armistice Day, 11 November, is a serious affair in France as well as a national holiday. At the eleventh hour, in my village, everyone gathers at the cenotaph in front of the church. This happens in villages, towns and cities all over France. The mayor lays a wreath and stands to attention alongside his deputy, who solemnly intones '*Mort pour la*

France', followed by the reading aloud of the names of villagers lost to war since the First World War. Alan Dundas Stewart, the twenty-one-year-old British soldier who died at the front, is also remembered, his name pronounced with a strong French accent. All is silent, other than cows mooing in the surrounding fields. It's a poignant and sombre event, one that brings the community together, and it always makes me cry. Afterwards, everyone meets at the town hall and the mayor pours a *vin d'honneur*, a glass of wine, to honour the memories of those lost.

The air starts to chill in November and generally it's a quiet month, as in much of the country, before the Christmas season kicks off. Local supermarkets stock great balls of wool for keen knitters, and there is a flutter of excitement on Beaujolais Nouveau Day – not always in a positive way. It's a tradition that has been around for more than fifty years, and producers of this *vin primeur* (young wine) race to get their wine onto the shelves of supermarkets and bars all over France and around the world (more than half the 25 million bottles produced head to the USA and Japan) for the third Thursday of November. Beaujolais Nouveau, a fruity red from Beaujolais in the east of France, has been around for centuries but the tradition of rushing it to outlets started in the 1950s. Then in the 1970s, a winemaker and businessman called Georges Duboeuf, who was also a major producer of Beaujolais Nouveau, started a publicity campaign. Banners proclaiming '*Le Beaujolais Nouveau est arrivé!*' became commonplace, and the race from Beaujolais to Paris gained ever-increasing media coverage each year with delivery methods becoming ever more exotic, including by Concorde, hot-air balloon and elephant. The legend of Beaujolais Nouveau Day seems to be more celebrated than the taste, which Jean-Claude describes as 'simple, with no depth, no complexity', though he never says *non* when I offer him a glass!

If you read the papers here you'll think that all French people loathe the tradition. Critics insist it's nothing more than a marketing operation, a cunning ploy to rid Burgundian winemakers of undrinkable wine in large quantities. Wine snobs claim they would rather down a bucket of cat wee.

And yet, to this day, wine bars and cafés all over France sport posters announce '*Le Beaujolais Nouveau est arrivé*', meaning that someone must be drinking it, and there aren't enough gullible foreign visitors or expats around to put away that much.

We were in Paris on Beaujolais Nouveau Day. We weren't there for the wine, but to celebrate my birthday. It's actually in September, but we'd had too much work to get away, what with the roof being mended, and we had to wait for someone to be able to babysit the animals. We're very lucky that despite living miles from anything, it only takes a few hours to drive to a station and take the train into the city. I have loved Paris since I stayed there as a fourteen-year-old exchange student with a family on the outskirts of the 13th Arrondissement. I remember being entranced by them drinking coffee from bowls, into which they also dunked their croissants. I've visited Paris many times since then, falling in love with each arrondissement, with hidden streets and secret squares, museums and markets, Notre Dame and the Eiffel Tower. Mark, on the other hand, was not such a fan. After one visit at the age of eighteen, when no one could understand his appalling French and declined to help him when he asked for directions, he had made up his mind that the hype about rude waiters, curt staff in shops and overcharging in restaurants was true. It didn't matter that I'd told him it was rubbish and no more particular to Paris than London or New York or any other city. But when he asked me what I wanted for my birthday, I told him I'd like to spend a weekend in Paris. I was determined to show him the Paris I know and love.

From Gare du Nord we took the Métro to Abbesses and Mark thought it would be a good idea to walk up the spiral stairs from the platforms to the surface. I've never done it before: most sane people take the lift at what is Paris's

the outside and as if it had been transplanted from 1965 on the inside. Dimly lit with low ceilings, its dark walls complemented dark wooden tables and chairs and, with feet falling off from the walking, we entered even though it was too early for dinner – no all-day meals here. The waiter invited us to sit and rest without so much as a hint of a '*pfff*' – the sound that French people make when they're at a loss for words at such a preposterous thing. He brought wine and olives over to us, and we sat and listened to two opera singers belt out numbers from *Carmen*.

At the end of our city sojourn, Mark was as much in love with Paris as I am. There is something about the city that's more than simply its architecture and the incredible culture there. Strolling, holding hands, through a freezing-cold park where *pétanque* was being played, drinking coffee that kept us awake all night and cocktails at a bar in Montparnasse where we met up with the Parisians, Hubert and Vava, we were struck by how many people we saw embracing, passionately kissing or just staring into each other's eyes. We vowed to one day live in Paris, if only for six months, although not with the animals. What Parisian neighbours would make of a couple of Brits with three dogs, five cats, nine ducks, four geese and thirty-eight chickens doesn't bear thinking about.

Back home, those ducks and chickens apparently spent half the time sheltering from the rain and the rest of the time making dirt baths in the chill winter sun, digging holes all over the garden for us to fall into on our return. There were more wild birds flocking to the bird feeders than I'd ever seen before – I even spotted two giant white storks in the field at the bottom of the garden. 'Sign of a bad winter,' reiterated Jean-Claude hopefully.

We'd never yet got through a winter without the pipes freezing. The November before we had a sudden and unexpected cold snap and only managed to thaw out the water to the kitchen after half an hour with a hair dryer aimed at pipes in the loft, keeping our fingers crossed that nothing would burst. But two weeks later, the pipes to the washing machine did burst and flooded the kitchen. We decided to insulate like we live in the Arctic, just in case one year Jean-Claude's prophecy of winter doom comes to pass.

One morning we dropped in on Monsieur and Madame Pepperpot to see if they needed help to move their cows for the winter. '*Oui, oui,*' they said, 'can you come tomorrow morning and have lunch afterwards?'

When we arrived the next day, the couple were ready, Madame Pepperpot with a thick coat over her housecoat, Monsieur with his cap pulled down against a steady stream of rain. In the field, it was almost as if the cows knew they were going somewhere different. They mooed loudly and started to wander off as the couple gently cajoled them and led them out of their small barn. We found ourselves forming a human passage to keep them on track and managed to get them into the back of a trailer. Monsieur had asked Mark if he could take it on the back of our 4 x 4, only to discover the trailer hitch was too big even for the tank. Monsieur phoned Thierry the farmer, who was providing winter lodging for the beasts. His wife Mathilde told us he was out in the field, but said that if Mark came up to their farm she would lend him a tractor as the cows shouldn't be left too long out in the cold.

Mark shot off only to return a while later, squashed into the cab of the tractor, with Mathilde at the wheel. He said he had looked at all the knobs and dials, and muttered something about space shuttles, so Mathilde had dropped off the child she was looking after and come herself to sort them out.

Inside the toasty farmhouse, which turned us cherry-cheeked, Madame Pepperpot ladled out bowls of scorching-hot cassoulet 'Toulouse style', rich with beans and sausage, covered with golden breadcrumbs. Served with hunks of baguette and a glass of red wine, it was enough to spark a love affair with the taste of the south. We felt pleasurably frozen in time and promised to come back and help when the Pepperpots returned from Toulouse after Christmas.

Although it may seem that we live in another century at times, with our lousy internet, lack of mains drains and no chance of ever being able to use a mobile phone at home, it might surprise you to know that 'Black Friday' arrived in middle-of-nowhere France in its own special way.

The shopping phenomenon that started in the US hasn't really been a big thing in France before now. The newspapers covered the event with relish '*C'est Quoi Black Friday?*' (What is Black Friday?) they asked, and then explained to the uninitiated French that it's the chance to spend loads of money to save loads of money. Retail experts predicted that it would cause an online spending spree in France. Not in our village, it wouldn't. The thought of all the mobile-phone confirmation codes generated by a consumer frenzy was enough to make us shiver, though I personally must have received about a million emails offering irresistible bargains. In Hucqueliers, however, they embraced the concept at the store where we buy chicken food; the week before Black Friday, after loading the sacks of bird food, dog food, cat food and wild-bird food into the tank (we buy at least 200 kg a month), the patron gave us a paper invitation to an evening of wine and duck sausage tart – plus 15 per cent off everything in the shop. 'We're calling it Green Friday on account of the fact that we sell things for the garden and for animals,' he explained.

'There's no obligation, just come and enjoy the tart and the wine, but if you want to buy, you'll save money – plus we've got some new cat treats in.' Clearly I can add Mad Cat Woman to my reputation as Madame Merde and Pig Lady.

The Wood Man, Monsieur Lassarat, came at the end of the month to drop off several tons of winter fuel. He'd delayed delivery until we had finished laying a new floor in the woodshed and, though we had a lot of Wood Club wood stacked in the back garden, we wanted to make sure we had enough to get through a long cold winter, just in case Jean-Claude's predictions were right.

Monsieur Lassarat is a big man who looks extremely unfit, with deep bags under his eyes and a heart condition. Despite this, he insists he doesn't want to retire and, though he leaves the heavy lifting to his son, a strapping young man who is as strong as a bull, he does all the deliveries in his old Fiat tipper truck and is the salesman for the firm, sweet-talking all of his customers. Like so many in these parts, he loves a chance to practise his English. I've lost count of the times I've read that in order to make friends in France you must speak good French. Obviously it helps, and without at least a modicum of French, dealing with the myriad administration departments that rule daily life can be a nightmare. But, on the whole, we have found that the majority of French people, even in the sticks where we are, speak a little English (Jean-Claude only knows swearwords, so he's not included). If you at least try to speak a little bit of French back, *entente cordiale* prevails. Just stock up on the *bon* words and use them a lot – *bonjour* (to everyone you meet), *bon appetit* (whenever you eat), *bonne journée, bon après-midi, bon soirée, bon dimanche, bonne anniversaire, bonnes vacances* and *bon courage* – use these liberally, and you'll do *bon*.

With three vanloads of wood dumped in front of the woodshed, ready for us to stack, the Wood Man came in for a coffee and to write out an invoice. Everything is on paper here – if you go to a market and buy a few bottles of wine, they'll probably give you an invoice, which will take longer to write than it did for you to choose your wine. When the Septic Tank Man (that's a highly unlikely name for a superhero) comes around, he too issues a paper invoice, which you are obliged to keep as proof that you've disposed of your vile contents responsibly and legally, instead of smearing them over the fields as some people used to do.

We chatted about the storm, Monsieur Lassarat trying to speak as much English as he could. I replied in French, as I often do, although I'm not sure why as it always results in a very confusing conversation. On the day of our biblical hailstorm, he was, he said, just 3 kilometres away from here and, though the sky darkened, there was not even a drop of rain. He came to look at our village afterwards and was horrified. Even now, it still looked like a disaster zone, but things were improving day by day.

He told me he had recently read a survey about the happiest places to live in France – we didn't do so well here in the north, and he wanted to know if I thought this was an unhappy place to live.

'Are you kidding?' I said. 'This region is amazing.'

The French can sometimes seem a morose bunch, and I think they secretly enjoy being miserable, at least in public. It's true that surveys and polls are always quoting that the French are generally not a happy-clappy crew and, compared to some other countries, they can be downright glum. I too had read about a world happiness index that reported that around 50 per cent of French respondents agreed that they were happy. Dig a little deeper, however, and it also stated that around 10 per cent said they were unhappy and a whopping 40 per cent ticked the 'neither happy nor unhappy' box, which definitely says something about the French psyche. My French is pretty good these days but explaining that to Monsieur Lassarat wasn't easy.

'Are you happy here?' I asked. He had to think about it. 'Well, it does rain quite a bit, but I don't really mind it, and it makes the flowers grow …'This went on: we don't have vineyards or make great wine, but we do have great beer. We don't have the most Michelin-starred restaurants, but we do have great food, amazing boulangeries and the best pâtisseries.

Monsieur Lassarat is, to me, a true representative of France – a paradox. On the one hand, he can seem full of *joie de vivre*, on the other, he's a little critical. And I find here in the north, they are pretty hard on themselves. I'm no scholar but in the majority of books and magazine articles about France, the focus is all on the chateaux of the Loire Valley, the monuments of Paris, the sunny south and its gastronomy, the wines of Burgundy, etc. It's bound to make you feel a bit like the underdog. The French tend to overthink things and that can make them somewhat gloomy. A frightfully clever French economist called Claudia Senik wrote, 'The fact of living in France reduces by twenty per cent the probability of declaring oneself very happy.'

I certainly don't need to take a survey to tell me whether this is a happy place to live.

Winter isn't a season, it's a feeling and a feast

SOMEONE IN A nearby village put their Christmas decorations up three weeks before the big day, which really got everyone talking. Normally you wouldn't even know it was Christmas here in the middle of nowhere until about three days before Christmas Day. Then people might put a simple, usually homemade holly wreath with bright berries and a sprinkling of mistletoe on the door, and perhaps a few twinkling lights strung around a tree in the garden. In my village, moderation with the decorations is the norm. It's been that way for centuries and no one is interested in changing it any time soon.

The offending house in question, two villages away, has multiple coloured lights arrayed around the windows as well as in the trees. There's even a life-sized inflatable reindeer and sleigh in the front garden, with a strangely out-of-proportion tiny inflatable Father Christmas holding onto the reins, a pained grimace on his painted plastic face. Despite the tendency towards minimal decoration, local people are keen on blow-up Father Christmases. They hang from the windows of houses and look like festive peeping Toms clutching onto windowsills – the plastic Santas, not the locals. They grip ropes tied to gutters and lampposts and swing wildly in the wind. I find it quite sad when I see a punctured Santa, deflated and drooping, the only sign of Christmas reduced to a piece of withered plastic.

Most of the regulars in one of our favourite local bars, near the little town of Fruges, are in agreement – three weeks before Christmas Day is simply too early for decorations. The bar is like being in someone's front room. There's a small gas fire set into a brown-tiled fireplace with a fifties vibe, and the room is lit by a few lamps on shelves. A TV set on a stand high up on the wall plays constantly, showing *le trot*, horse-and-cart racing, which is wildly popular, or the winning numbers of the lottery draw. It's rather dark in the bar; the walls are an indeterminate dull brown, and the wooden tables and chairs have seen better days. Madame the proprietor is short with a blonde beehive hairdo, which I suspect she may have had since the sixties. Her little Jack Russell, which is trapped behind a half door, yaps and tries to get out to lick customers and nibble their shoes. She does a brisk business when she's open, which seems to be at quite random times based on when she feels like it. Apart from being a bar it's also where you can buy lottery tickets, tobacco products and fishing tackle as well as pocket knives and chewing gum. But what makes it special is Madame and the friendly regulars. When you walk in, even if you are a complete stranger, everyone says hello, many shake your hand and when you leave they all say goodbye. It might not be that glamorous, but it's cosy and makes you feel like you belong.

Coming up to Christmas, Madame always announces with great pride that she will be decorating the bar 'early' this year – precisely five days before the day itself. No one is particularly excited by this, since her idea of festive embellishment consists of little plastic, movement-activated dancing Father Christmas dolls, which she places on tables and the traditional zinc counter alongside the porcelain beer pumps. When you walk past them, the little Santas twitch as if in the final throes of their existence, accompanied by a faint sound of tinny, washed-out music. We all tiptoe round the bar in an effort not to set them off.

'Well,' says Monsieur Lafont, who likes to think he is the font of all knowledge, 'personally I think those people in that village are a bit crazy to have put their decorations up this early. They won't last. The first gust of strong wind and that reindeer will be over the trees, up the hill and off to Paris!'

Everyone nods at his sage words; it wouldn't do to have anything go to Paris, after all. 'It's bad enough that the president and his wife have a home in our department,' he adds. 'Every time they come to stay, there are traffic jams because of paparazzi. It's not right, you know.' This is enough to set everyone off on another discussion topic: is it a good thing to have celebrities living in your area? The consensus is that if Angelina Jolie wants to come and live here in the middle of nowhere now that she and Brad Pitt are no longer together, no one would mind. We are all fairly sure that she would put her Christmas decorations up early, but in her case we would allow it.

With just over a week until Christmas Day, we were invited to a soirée at the home of Madame Bernadette, who would be spending Christmas in the south of France with some of her family. The invitation said 7 p.m., so naturally we got there for 7.30. There was no sign of Christmas cheer from the outside of her house – of course, there were still several days to go before that could happen.

In the little farmhouses of my village you generally open the front door and find yourself in the main room of the house, where everyone spends the most time. At Madame

Bernadette's, that's a large kitchen, the warmest room in the house, heated by a huge coal and wood oven. Coming in from the crisp night air under bright stars sparkling alongside a full moon, walking over ground twinkling with frost – it was sweltering. The wall of heat instantly misted up my glasses, leaving me momentarily disorientated in the steamy haze. Madame Bernadette had the perfect answer to that – a chilled cocktail made with Calvados. If you've never had Calvados before, be warned – this apple brandy from Normandy, the region that neighbours mine, can blow your socks off. And, I have to tell you, we were all pretty much sockless after a couple of hours.

There were about twenty-five of us in total, with Mark and me being the only Brits. Usually we find it hard to keep up with the rapid French conversation of these northerners, but I think the Calvados helped (it may well be the future for language learners). I once went to Caen in Normandy to be a judge of Calvados cocktails for an annual event which sees the top bar staff from around the world gather together to showcase the mixes we'll all be sipping in the future. I was judging the amateur entries created by international journalists attending the event. We began with a breakfast workshop, tasting different types of Calvados, and in the afternoon I had to taste twenty different cocktails made from Calvados and vegetables, the theme for the year. Let's just say some concoctions were better than others but an unexpected side effect was that it cured my cold and I seemed to be able to speak French like a native.

Most of the other guests were from the village. There are fewer than 150 residents in total and we all live within minutes of each other. We pretty much know everyone by sight, if not by name. Even after several years of living here, the older residents still like to be called monsieur or madame instead of by their Christian name. This does not mean you don't kiss them, though. Puckering up twenty-five times certainly builds up a thirst, which inevitably leads to more Calvados cocktails.

Four jolly farmers from the next village along arrived after us, stamping their feet on the mat as they entered and rubbing freezing-cold hands together – it's a brisk fifteen-minute walk from their small hamlet. Soft music played in the background – something very French with a male singer of gravelly voice, perhaps Charles Aznavour (he has never gone out of fashion here). People were talking and laughing, helping themselves to delicious little pastries and canapés that Madame Bernadette had prepared earlier in the day. Delicate little melt-in-your-mouth choux buns filled with fresh, tangy goats cheese from the Goat Lady's farm. Mini tartelettes filled with smoky lardons and onion confit. Delicate golden *gougères* like crunchy balloons flavoured with salty and nutty Comté cheese from eastern France. Tender mini-croquettes with silky tomato coulis, saucisson and blue cheese. And, *petite foie gras* and redcurrant jam lollipops, like miniature shiny crimson works of art. Madame Bernadette beamed as everyone licked their lips in appreciation of her cooking skills.

Wood Club member Monsieur Rohart risked a risqué joke. It earned him a look from his wife that was probably intended to turn him to stone. But, the Calvados seemed to make him bold, so rather than look contrite, he flashed her a charming smile that would melt the heart of most women. No such luck with Madame Rohart, however – his spouse of thirty years glared and accepted another cocktail from Madame Bernadette without taking her eyes off her errant husband. Twenty-three sets of eyebrows were raised, as we all knew that tomorrow one or several of our homes would be sure to get a visit from him, keen to escape his nagging wife.

Jean-Claude and Bernadette brought with them an enormous *bûche de Noël*, a Christmas yule-log cake, made by a master pâtissier in Le Touquet, which, though a small town, has half a dozen outstanding cakeshops. Decorated with chocolate to look like a real log, it had sprigs of holly made from marzipan and sugar-crafted miniature champagne bottles spraying tiny sugar bubbles.

A 1950s drinks cabinet had as its centrepiece a glass bowl of homemade crème de menthe, which nobody touched except Petit Frère. We had all heard the story of the man from a village two miles away who once drank an entire glass of locally made mint-green liqueur and woke up two days later.

At around midnight people started to go home. We were just about to leave when we heard the sound of a noisy tractor revving up outside. 'Aha,' cried the jolly famers who were rather jollier now than when they had first arrived, 'Sam is here.' They pulled on their boots and coats, kissed everyone goodbye and trooped out the door.

We followed behind and watched as they climbed into the big metal box on the back of the tractor-turned-country-taxi, and Sam, the designated driver, lurched off up the road, smoke belching from the vehicle's exhaust. The jolly farmers were singing songs and clinging to each other, doing their best not to fall off the back of the tractor. We could just about make out their happy faces in the yellow glow of the moon.

The party marked the start of the festive season, which is almost entirely centred on food. If you're on a diet, don't go to France at Christmas. When it comes to the scrumptious treats, temptation is everywhere. Any time you visit is likely to be the start of a gastronomic affair, to be honest, but in winter even more so. Recipes are shared with fervour and news of the arrival of fresh winter squash at a market travels fast.

When the Bread Man arrived that month with his normal vanload of bread and croissants, he also brought traditional Christmas treats. *Craquelin boulonnais*, which originated from the city of Boulogne-sur-Mer, is a pastry shaped in a figure of eight that's a cross between a sugary pretzel and a croissant, but with even more butter, which hardly seems possible. If that's not bad enough, people here like to dip them into a bowl of treacle-thick hot chocolate. And a local Christmas cake called a *coquille*. It has been made in the far north of France since at least the sixteenth century. It's not for the faint-hearted – a large, sweet brioche bun filled with butter, sugar and raisins, and yes, just looking at one makes you put on weight. Spicy gingerbread fills the van with sweet smells, and there are crispy cookies iced with the smiling face of Saint Nicholas. *Galette des rois* cakes, which are traditionally eaten for the Epiphany on 6 January when the Three Kings turned up to give gifts to the baby Jesus, creep onto shopping lists a few weeks before the day. Within this sweet, flaky and buttery frangipane tart, bakers hide a charm called a *fève*, which can be anything from a mini religious figure to a Disney figure to a celebrity. Whoever gets the charm in their slice of cake tries not to break a tooth or swallow it, and is then 'crowned' king or queen with a paper crown that comes with the cake. Apparently the president doesn't need to worry about that, as he's not allowed to have a charm in his *galette*.

The Bread Man's English had improved considerably during the last few months, aided by watching American TV programmes with his daughter. Handing over my baguette and a *craquelin* (you can only get them at this time of the year, that's my excuse), he tells me that his daughter Nadia has asked him to ask me, 'What is sucks?'

'Pardon?' I ask warily, wondering what on earth she has been watching.

'Nadia says that Americans say it a lot. *Buffy the Vampire Slayer, The Mentalist* and Abby on *NCIS*, they say "that sucks" all the time.'

Phew. This, I could explain. 'When you're not happy with something, you say it sucks,' I said. 'Like if you leave the bread in the oven too long and the baguette is burned, you could say that sucks.' I looked down at my dark brown and very crispy baguette.

'Like we would say *ça ne casse pas trois pattes à un canard*?' Literally this is 'it doesn't break three of a duck's legs', but means 'it's nothing to write home about'. It is one of those phrases that makes me think that, however much my

French improves, there's a long way still to go. That and asking where the rubber gloves (*gants en caoutchouc*) are in the supermarket. When I say the almost impossible to pronounce '*caoutchouc*', it sounds more like 'cow shit' and makes Mark laugh every time.

'Not quite, it's more like *ça craint* or, if it sucks a lot, *c'est nul*,' I said, just as the post lady arrived clutching a bundle of calendars, which are sold for Christmas tips.

'*Ah merci*,' said the Bread Man. ''Appy Christmas.' He chuckled to himself and mumbled 'Ze brrrread sucks' as he got into his van to drive off to Madame Bernadette, who was waiting impatiently at the gate of her little cottage down the bottom of the hill, ready to scrutinize the baskets of Christmassy cakes.

Shopping for Christmas food in France requires time, planning and *savoir faire* – knowing where to get the best of everything is important. Supermarkets are full of the sound of largely English-language Christmas songs and shelves are heaving with all manner of treats – wine, champagne and liqueurs. There's even Christmas beer, a strong and fruity brew. Boxes of oysters are sold at a rate of knots at markets, bringing with them an odour of the seaside. Cakeshops in the towns will vie for custom, their windows crammed with enticing pastries, and perfectly illustrating why the French call window shopping *lèche-vitrine* – window licking! Cheese shops will do a roaring trade, and baguettes and breads of all sorts will be zipping out of the boulangerie doors as bakers bake furiously to try to keep up with demand.

Christmas markets are one of the most popular places for finding seriously mouth-watering treats with stallholders popping up from all around France selling local products such as cognac from Cognac, Chablis from Chablis and champagne from Champagne. Not to mention cheeses from all over the country, foie gras, crystallized fruit, tasty tapenade and other goodies from Provence, cheesy tarts from the Haute-Savoie region and great steaming tubs of Alsatian *choucroute* (sauerkraut). Every town holds a Christmas market. It might be for an afternoon or daily for five weeks. Shopping while you wander streets and squares sparkling with lights, the aroma of hot chestnuts and mulled wine hanging in the cold air, is one of winter's great pleasures in northern France.

We headed to the annual Christmas market at Boulogne-sur-Mer where the shops were decked with lights and the ancient UNESCO listed belfry was lit up. Little wooden chalets were festooned with festive wreaths, manned by smiling artisans, unbothered by the rain as the cobbled streets around them glistened with water. A four-man band roamed the street playing happy tunes alongside jugglers and elves. Knights cantered around on wooden hobby horses, entertaining the crowd and, discovering I was *Anglaise*, made me repeat phrases that I didn't remotely understand. I was probably saying things such as 'I am a boiled egg' or 'I like to eat worms.' Whatever it was, it certainly got a good laugh from the by now large audience watching me blush at being the centre of attention.

On Christmas Eve, the emphasis is firmly on feasting and family, and tables are laden with all those gourmet delicacies that took such effort to seek out. The long, long *réveillon* dinner lasts until the early hours of Christmas morning. All over the village dishes will be made with love and passion as keen cooks prepare for the evening's festivities. Around midnight, a DJ will arrive at the town-hall party room and the more youthful residents will leave the family table to join their friends for a shindig, while the elders with any stamina left remain at the table. Owls will hoot in indignation, appalled by the sound of the throbbing music from the bottom of the hill.

Christmas Day is quieter in these parts and some boulangeries even open in the morning so that people can get their can't-live-without-it fresh bread. For us, it's a day for exploring empty beaches with the dogs, wrapped against the cold, running up and down mountainous sand dunes and thanking our lucky stars for all that we have.

Next day, everything goes back to normal, no Boxing

Day holiday here in France. Shops open as usual and even the dustmen come to empty the bins. But it's not like any other week since New Year's Eve is on the doorstep and that means preparation for the next banquet begins …

On New Year's Eve we went to wish Claudette *bonne fin d'année* (you don't say *bonne année,* happy new year, here until the first day of January) before we had to get ready for the evening's festivities. It was a freezing afternoon and everyone had their shutters firmly closed, making the village look like a ghost town except for the wisps of smoke coming from chimneypots. The pale winter sun was just disappearing behind the hill where Monsieur's white horses stood out against the still verdant grass. Rosy hues lit up the sky, mist hovered over the fields, and great balls of mistletoe like giant nests made by the world's biggest birds stood out in the leafless trees. There was so much mistletoe that even the Christmas culling had made no discernible difference. Thierry's sheepdog came hurtling down the hill to see where we were going and followed us into Claudette's courtyard.

'*Entrez,*' called Claudette when we knocked, and hot air blasted out as we pushed open the door. Hurrying in, we were ushered straight to the kitchen table, as is the way when you visit people here. A glass of wine was poured before we could get our coats off, the oven was stoked up and the dog, which had followed us in, was told to stay by the fire. He was clearly used to sneaking in to keep company with the old lady.

'Would you like something to eat?' asked Claudette. 'No thanks,' I said, which was pointless because Claudette takes no notice and always puts food on the table when someone arrives. Out came a little dish of homemade spiced walnuts, slices of saucisson, little rounds of baguette, a pat of salty butter on a wooden board and some tiny madeleine cakes.

'Now,' she said as she sat down, 'how is your next book coming along, Janine? Mark, what will you be working on next? We are betting it won't be long before you are building something new! Drink your wine ... try those nuts ...'

She gabbled away in fast French, her rural accent as strong as ever, and before we knew it, an hour had gone by as we chatted about this and that. People here are not rich, but in terms of kindness, of caring and of neighbourliness, Mark and I really feel like we hit the jackpot when, by fate and pure luck, we discovered a neglected farmhouse in a tiny village no one has ever heard of.

Also by Janine Marsh

MY GOOD LIFE IN FRANCE:
IN PURSUIT OF THE RURAL DREAM

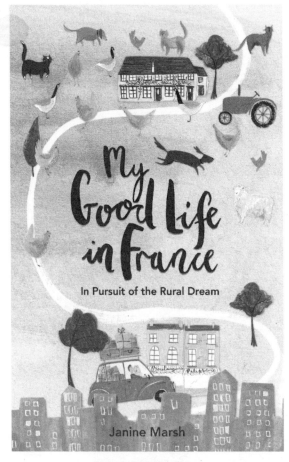

978-1-78243-732-1

£8.99

Available in paperback, ebook and audiobook formats